How To
Climb 5.12

"The best book of its type I have read yet (and I've read 'em all, I think)."
—Dr. Mark Robinson

"Concise, informative and easily digestible. Super effort and super job, Eric!"
—Steve Petro

"Well researched and right on."
—Lynn Hill

◆ HOW TO ROCK CLIMB SERIES ◆

How To
Climb 5.12!

Eric J. Hörst

CHOCKSTONE

FALCON®

2 3 4 5 6 7 8 9 0 VP 04 03 02 01 00

COVER PHOTO: Lisa Ann Hörst on "King Me" (5.11c), Red River Gorge, Kentucky. Photo by Mike McGill

BACK COVER PHOTO: by Mike McGill

Cataloging-in-Publication data is on record at the Library of Congress.

All other photographs by the author unless otherwise credited.

ISBN 1-57540-083-9

DISTRIBUTED BY:
Falcon Publishing Co., Inc.
P.O. Box 1718
Helena, Montana 59624

PUBLISHED BY:
Chockstone Press

OTHER BOOKS IN THIS SERIES:
How to Rock Climb!
Climbing Anchors
Advanced Climbing
Sport Climbing
Big Walls
Flash Training!
Knots for Climbers
Nutrition for Climbers
Building Your Own Indoor Climbing Wall
Gym Climb
Clip and Go!
Self Rescue
More Climbing Anchors
Top Roping
How To Ice Climb!

Acknowledgements

How to Climb 5.12!

ERIC J. HÖRST

I would like to thank everyone who in some way contributed to or helped produce *How to Climb 5.12*. Excellent photography and artwork grace the pages throughout—thanks to Stewart Green, Peter Lewis, Mike McGill, Michael Miller, Carl Samples, Rick Thompson, Eddie Whittemore, and Sean Michael. A few gyms and climbers enthusiastically helped in producing the instructional photos—thanks to Climbnasium, Philadelphia Rock Gym, and Vertical Extreme, and to Bob Africa, John Boschetti, L. A. Hörst, Matt Kellerman, Scott Mechler, Tom Muller, Brinda Salla, and Bruce Stick. Also, many thanks to Russ Clune, Mark Robinson, Steve Petro, Jay McElwain, Andrzej Malewicz, and Bob Perna for the early read throughs and invaluable feedback. And to the companies who support me and my efforts—NICROS, La Sportiva, and Chockstone Press—you are all great.

Finally, to my wife Lisa Ann and to my parents—thanks for unconditional love, support, and late-night proofreading. Thanks to my training partners and the hometown buys, LIVE, for the best training tunes around! And to Gayle and Dave Plecha for the post-writing refuge in RPV.

Dedicated to my brother, Kyle, for introducing me to this outrageous sport!

WARNING: CLIMBING IS A SPORT WHERE YOU MAY BE SERIOUSLY INJURED OR DIE

READ THIS BEFORE YOU USE THIS BOOK.

This is an instruction book to rock climbing, a sport which is inherently dangerous. You should not depend solely on information gleaned from this book for your personal safety. Your climbing safety depends on your own judgment based on competent instruction, experience, and a realistic assessment of your climbing ability.

There is no substitute for personal instruction in rock climbing and climbing instruction is widely available. You should engage an instructor or guide to learn climbing safety techniques. If you misinterpret a concept expressed in this book, you may be killed or seriously injured as a result of the misunderstanding. Therefore, the information provided in this book should be used only to supplement competent personal instruction from a climbing instructor or guide. Even after you are proficient in climbing safely, occasional use of a climbing instructor is a safe way to raise your climbing standard and learn advanced techniques.

There are no warranties, either expressed or implied, that this instruction book contains accurate and reliable information. There are no warranties as to fitness for a particular purpose or that this book is merchantable. Your use of this book indicates your assumption of the risk of death or serious injury as a result of climbing's risks and is an acknowledgement of your own sole responsibility for your climbing safety.

Rick Thompson on "Crimes of Flashin'" (5.12a), New River Gorge, West Virginia.
Photo: Carl Samples

HOW TO CLIMB 5.12!

ERIC J. HÖRST

C O N T E N T S

*Mark Van Cura on
"Clean Crack" (5.11),
Squamish, British
Columbia.*

Photo: Carl Samples

Introduction

A better title for this book might be How to Get Good, Fast! After all, that's the obsession of participants in most sports, whether a golfer searching for par or a runner in quest of the four-minute mile. In the sport of climbing, 5.12 has become known as the sort of "door" to elite levels. For years 5.12 ascents were a rare feat achieved by few. Although more common today, 5.12 is still a magical grade, and chances are you have what it takes to get there. But how can you get there most quickly?

With the recent glut of climbing books on the market it's hard to find time to digest and utilize all the material. Although I'm adding to that glut with this book, *How to Climb 5.12* offers a fresh, streamlined approach to increasing your performance on the rock—fast!

The following pages serve up much of what I've learned during my second decade in this sport. The material ranges from long-held absolutes on fitness training to cutting-edge methods for honing technique to proven tips on redpointing difficult projects. You may recognize some of the ideas from previous readings, but there is much you'll read here for the first time. I've reviewed volumes of university research on motor learning and sport performance, conducted many interviews with top climbers, and spent countless days experimenting and developing new training methods (when I should have been out climbing). Much of that material appears on the pages of this book and has been edited down for clarity and brevity.

Life is short. You should aim at what you feel the most like doing.

—Patrick Edlinger

Although this book covers dozens of skill, fitness, and mental training techniques, it does not offer in-depth instruction on specific moves or exercises. Consult John Long's *How to Rock Climb* and *Sport Climbing* for excellent and entertaining technical instruction. For a more comprehensive review of climbing performance, I suggest both Dale Goddard's *Performance Rock Climbing* and my first book for Chockstone Press, *Flash Training*.

Finally, I want to comment that I was a bit hesitant to use the 5.12 grade in the title of this book. I'm a firm believer that the difficultly of a climb is secondary to the simple pleasure of pulling down on some good rock. However, it would be a lie to say that the lust to climb ever-more-difficult routes is not a strong motivator for most. Breaking barriers, achieving dreams, and the intense rush of doing an outrageous route is part of the spirit of this sport. And it is killer fun!

With this in mind, I want to add that your trip to 5.12 (and beyond) must always be fun. If it ever starts to feel like a job, then it's time to take a few weeks off. Savor the successes, failures, and hard work during your journey. Drop me a note when you send your first 5.12. Enjoy the road trip!

15 year old David Hume
on Vitamin H (5.12c/d),
Rifle, Colorado.
Photo: Stewart Green

Yes, You Can Climb 5.12!

Climbing is an incredibly complex sport. It's not just a matter of strength. There are mental factors to consider as well as motivation, technique, experience and confidence.

—Tony Yaniro

If you are reading this book, chances are you have what it takes to climb 5.12.

Whatever your age or occupation, most climbers I meet have the potential to succeed at this difficult grade. I know a 14-year-old girl and a 60-plus-year-old gentleman (who underwent double bypass surgery a few years back) who currently redpoint 5.12. I also know a number of teachers, laborers, two contractors, several doctors, a chef, a tailor, a restaurant manager, a couple doctoral thesis students, even a librarian who regularly climb 5.12. Undoubtedly, you can be added to this list. (Let me know, and I'll put you on!)

The two things stopping most people from reaching the grade are lack of accurate information on how to get there and periodic lapses in motivation, desire, or discipline. Although the latter items have to come from inside you, the how-to-get-there information is available in heavy doses right here, right now.

GETTING "ON ROUTE" TO 5.12

Most people unknowingly get "lost" long before reaching 5.12 due to a combination of trial-and-error learning and misinformation. Ultimately, this approach will have you climbing to a dead end.

As a metaphor, suppose you wanted to climb the Nose of El Capitan in Yosemite but had no guidebook, beta, line of fixed gear, or chalk to follow. All you knew was that the climb went somewhere up the literal nose of El Cap. How successful would you be? Initially, you'd probably succeed at getting a pitch or two off the ground "somewhere" on the nose. Your confidence would skyrocket as you figure to be on route! Right? But looming above are many cracks and corners. Which to take now? Do you need to pendulum to another line? Unfortunately, without an accurate guide you'd never know the correct route up. Progress slows and eventually you hit a dead end.

This scenario parallels the story line of many a climber's journey toward 5.12. Huge amounts of invested energy and time result in ever-decreasing gains in ability. Eventually, progress becomes negligible as climbing ability plateaus short of 5.12.

LIVING IN THE INFORMATION AGE

In an effort to break through the plateau, it's natural to want to seek and load up on any information and advice you can wring out of other climbers. Some common advice you are likely to hear: "Wear tighter shoes, climb a lot, do lots of pull-ups, join a gym, work on projects, get even tighter shoes, do more pull-ups, eat fewer calories and lose weight, do more pull-ups, hang on a fingerboard, train harder, climb some more, train even harder, buy some campus rungs, eat even less, climb even more...."

Unfortunately, this mindless, shoot-from-the-hip approach will yield about the same results as trying to climb El Cap without a guidebook. It lacks an intelligent plan based on facts and it suffers from the childish mentality that "if some is good, more must be better." If climbing three days a week is good, then climbing six days a week is twice as good. If dieting is good, then a crash diet is better. Obviously, these theories are flawed, but there are a surprising number of climbers enamored of them.

The good news is that since we're all human beings there are certain facts and theories that apply equally to us all. In medicine, a vaccine that works on one human being will work on all human beings. Or with respect to diet, if I eat more calories than I burn, I will get fat, and if you eat more calories than you burn, you will get fat. Likewise, there are training absolutes and motor learning theories (about how we acquire complex skills) that are valid for all human beings. If we understand these principles and follow them, then we will get similar results.

Certainly, we all have unique DNA that defines each of us.

Nine Absolute Truths of Climbing Performance

1. The best training for climbing skill (technique and tactics) is climbing.
2. Climbing skills are specific to the rock type, angle, and frictional properties.
3. Skills practice yields a greater return-on-investment than fitness training for all but elite climbers.
4. General conditioning is the most effective type of fitness training for beginner-level climbers.
5. Sport-specific conditioning is the most effective fitness training for advanced climbers.
6. Strength training builds endurance, but endurance training does not build maximum strength.
7. Wasted energy and time are lost forever.
8. Your body cannot go where the mind has not gone first.
9. Training and climbing provide stimulus for, but no actual, muscular growth. Recomposition and strengthening occur only during sleep and rest days.

We all have slightly different potential, which means different starting and ending points in terms of absolute climbing ability. But I believe the "end point" of the envelope of potential is beyond 5.12a for most individuals!

Detailed below are nine absolutes of climbing performance that provide a foundation for this text. In the following chapters, you'll see these absolutes give birth to many subprinciples and practice techniques that are supremely effective. Develop your training program accordingly, and the trip to 5.12 will be faster than you think!

NINE ABSOLUTE TRUTHS OF CLIMBING PERFORMANCE

Absolute #1: The best training for climbing skill (technique and tactics) is climbing.

This first absolute might seem obvious, but it surprises me how many people act in a manner contrary to this principle. The concept of cross-training does not apply to sport skills as complex as climbing. Time spent doing any other sport with the thought that it "might help my climbing" is time wasted. I have yet to find a sport with technical and tactical requirements anywhere similar to climbing.

Although there may be some minor transfer of the fitness conditioning gained by doing other sports, there will be no gain in skill. Even activities that seem to have something in common to climbing (like the balance required for gymnastics or walking a slack chain) transfer no skill to the vertical plane.

Sure, variety is the spice of life. However, if your goal is to

"A Virgin No More" (5.12c/d), Penitente, Colorado.

photo: Stewart Green

become an ace on the rock, it's your time spent climbing that will get you there. Invest what play time you have on this sport and dabble in all the rest only on your days off or during rest periods between training cycles.

Absolute #2: Climbing skills are specific to rock type, angle, and frictional properties.

Climbing may be a "natural" activity, but the skills required for proficiency in this sport are as complex as any other. There are literally thousands of different climbing areas with likely millions of different routes. Each route possesses slightly different character and form requiring you to execute somewhat different techniques and tactics in every case.

Climbing movements may be similar from one climb to the next, but the actual moves feel different due to variations in rock type, angle, and frictional properties. Skill is therefore very sensitive/specific to the infinite variations in our "playing field." You have lived the proof of this principle, I'm sure.

We're all familiar with the phenomena of the indoor "prince of plastic" who instantly transforms into a pauper on real rock (the opposite is also common). People who excel on slab climbs are often mediocre on vertical or overhanging rock. You may even know a local "rock star" who can shred 5.11s on his turf but gets spanked on 5.10s while on a road trip. The classic example is the crack master who flails on face climbs, and the sport climber who couldn't jam a hand-crack for a million bucks.

Of course, the best climbers perform well in almost any situation and at most areas. They climb at an exceedingly high level because they have "programmed" gazillions of different moves that are on call at a moment's notice. Consequently, they can react quickly, and often intuitively to even the most novel moves and sequences. This is your goal, and climbing at many different areas is the means. Start driving.

Absolute #3: Skills practice yields a greater return-on-investment than fitness training for all but elite climbers.

The learning curve for climbing skill is steeper and continues upward longer and more steadily than a curve showing gains in climbing strength from fitness training. Period. If you have a limited amount of time to invest in training and climbing, it would be wise to use that time actually climbing instead of fitness training.

In business it's called return on investment. It goes like this: You have $100 to invest on two possible investments. One guarantees a pay back of $200 in just one month, the other may pay back $125...if you're lucky. Where do you put your money? Should you split it between the two? Of course not. Put it all in the first investment!

In climbing, training skill is the sure-fire investment. Like the first investment in the previous example, steady gains are guaranteed. Time put into strength training (like investment two above) may yield gradual gains but with nowhere near the rate and certainty of training skill.

Elite climbers with highly honed skills are the exception. Their investment "money" is better placed on strength training (due to some strange market force!).

Absolute #4: General conditioning is the most effective type of fitness training for beginner-level climbers.

Okay, so you're a beginner-level climber with the time and desire to do some strength training. Invest your time in becoming an all-around well-conditioned physical specimen such as Lynn Hill or Tony Yaniro, not an Arnold lookalike (Tom or Schwarzenegger!). Your goal is to minimize body fat and unnecessary muscle mass, as both will pull you down. You also want to tune up all your muscles, particularly those used in pulling motions. Perform a moderate amount of aerobic training—running is ideal—to drop the fat and reduce bulky muscles. Or if you're more "Twiggy-like," begin some low-resistance circuit or free weight training two or three days per week.

For now, don't worry about developing fingers of steel. Sport-specific exercises such as fingerboards, Bachar ladder, and campus training are inappropriate at this time and may result in injury.

Absolute #5: Sport-specific conditioning is the most effective fitness training for advanced climbers.

The most difficult routes often require heroic feats of strength in situations where even God-like technique isn't enough to win. If you're very solid on 5.10 and possess all-around conditioning and technique, then some sport-specific strength training should be added to your program. Increased pulling power and a vice-like grip are your goals.

Cut back or eliminate general conditioning and focus your fitness training time on the pursuit of maximum strength in the arms and forearms. Progress deep into the 5.12 grade depends on it.

Absolute #6: Strength training builds endurance, but endurance training does not build maximum strength.

Your sport-specific fitness training must focus first and foremost on building maximum strength, particularly in the arms and forearms. Obviously, with this higher level of strength you will be better prepared for the most savage crux sequences. But that's not all. On the many submaximal moves throughout the rest of a climb, you'll be able to use a lower percentage of maximum strength. This means more endurance!

Unfortunately, improved endurance will not benefit your maximum strength even 1 percent. It comes down to return on your training investment. In this case, the big money lies in training maximum strength.

Absolute #7: Wasted energy and time are lost forever.

The quickest way to increase apparent strength and endurance is not through training but by reducing wasted energy while climbing. Of course, it's impossible to quantify the amount of energy the average climber needlessly expends on a route; I would guess it's in the ballpark of 50 percent. If I'm anywhere close on this estimation, there's a huge windfall of strength awaiting the climber who makes a conscious effort to end this "overcharge."

Your climbing skill (technique and tactics), or lack there-of, is at the heart of this matter. Climb too slow, grip too hard, use poor body positioning, miss a hold, and you'll use far

Mike McGill on Rose de Sables, Buoux, France.

more energy than required. This highlights the value of Absolute #3 that states the high importance of training skill.

Your mind is also a powerful tool in the quest to conserve energy. Acute awareness of energy "leaks" and poise in the midst of battle are two characteristics of champion climbers. Reaching 5.12 will be difficult and painful without them.

Absolute #8: Your body cannot go where the mind has not gone first.

Visualization is used by almost every elite athlete, in every sport, in every country. Period. Whether it's Carl Lewis visualizing a winning long jump or François Legrand visualizing another world-cup climbing win, success cannot come without it.

Visualization prepares a mental blueprint for action and thus the framework for reality. It must be as factual, detailed, and positive if it is to give birth to the desired results. Certainly many failures have been preprogrammed by poor-quality visualization based on erroneous information, negative thoughts, and unreasonable fears. Only through daily use in a wide range of applications will you master this skill.

Begin using visualization before all important tasks whether a speech at school, a job at work, or a fix-up at home. Create a full-color mental movie of the best course of action, and always end it with a vivid image of the ideal outcome.

Home walls are great, but also very tempting. Stick to a prearranged workout schedule and take lots of rest days.

Absolute #9: Training and climbing provide stimulus for, but no actual, muscular growth. Recomposition and strengthening occur only during sleep and on rest days.

Your muscles become stronger and your nervous system adapts to new moves and demands during rest periods not during exercise. Although climbing and training are the stimulus for growth, they are actually catabolic, meaning they break down your body. Therefore, the quality and quantity of your recovery time is as important as your training and climbing time.

Supercompensation requires specific macro nutrients as

well as vitamins and minerals. At least three square meals a day, nine hours of sleep each night, and two to three days off are required to elevate your strength higher than before the workout. However, climb too much, sleep too little, skip meals, and eat junk and your abilities will straightline. Overtraining is the ultimate bad investment because it yields negative returns, and frequently, injury or sickness.

Nine Absolute Tips

1. Always favor climbing as training over nonspecific exercises such as those at a health club. (See Chapter 2 for details.)
2. Travel to and pull down on as many different types of rock as possible to expand your "library" of moves. This will put you on the fast track to 5.12. (See Chapter 2 for details.)
3. Favor skill practice over strength training at a ratio of 3 to 1. The exception are elite climbers who may benefit most from at 1 to 2 ratio. (See Chapter 2 for details.)
4. Beginner-level climbers should perform mainly general fitness training. Avoid sport-specific exercises during the first few months to a year in this sport. (See Chapter 3 for details.)
5. Advanced climbers must plan and execute a smart, sound sport-specific training program to break through plateaus and reach the higher grades. (See Chapter 3 for details.)
6. Focus sport-specific strength training, particularly of the fingers, on building maximum strength, instead of endurance. (See Chapter 3 for details.)
7. Work for acute awareness of wasted energy and time, whether in the gym or on the rock. Honing your technical and mental skills will yield a windfall of strength you thought you never had. (See Chapters 2 and 4 for details.)
8. Practice visualization daily in a wide variety of everyday activities. In climbing, use visualization when working on new moves, before every climb, in competition, and even while training. This enhances learning and increases the likelihood of success. (See Chapter 4 for details.)
9. Value rest time and quality nutrition as much as time you spend training. Increase rest volume in proportion to increases in your training intensity. (See Chapter 3 for details.)

EVALUATING YOUR CURRENT PERFORMANCE

Your quest for 5.12 must incorporate constant evaluations and re-evaluations to determine your climbing-related strengths, weaknesses, and desires. Strengths are easy to sort out because it's human nature to think about and practice the things at which you are good. Unfortunately, identifying your weaknesses is quite difficult and might not be your idea of a good time. It is necessary, though, if you want to keep your performance curve rising toward 5.12.

A friend or instructor's objective evaluation is a great place to start—he or she may be able to identify obvious flaws in technique, tactics, and the like. For example, feet scraping at or popping off footholds signals lack of attention to footwork, and constant stretching for holds out of reach are signs of missed intermediate hand or foot holds and bad sequencing.

However, some fundamental mistakes and weaknesses are subtle and not easily observed. Things such as overgripping holds, holding your breath, high anxiety, poor visualization, and inability to quickly figure out sequences are difficult to diagnose from the ground. A detailed self-assessment is the ticket here. Self-assessment takes the "white light" of your climbing performance and breaks it into a spectrum of colors representing specific skills. It highlights your strengths and weaknesses and may reveal your hidden Achilles' heal. Only then can you develop a strategic plan for achieving peak performance.

Take the Self-Assessment Test on page 12. Read each question once and immediately answer it based on your recent experiences on the rock. Don't read anything into the questions or try to figure out its focus or the "best" answer. When totaling your scores, you'll see that each question focuses on either mental, technical/tactical, or physical skills. A perfect score would be 25 points in all three areas of focus. However, keep in mind that the goal of this assessment is to identify weaknesses. It's the low-scoring questions and "focus area" we are most interested in, as they hold the keys to unlocking higher levels of performance.

Finally, I urge you not to compare your score with anyone else. Such a comparison is meaningless, since we all hold ourselves to a different standard when taking such self-analysis tests.

Whether you are a beginner or a Nationals competitor like Chris Sharma, you must critique your performance regularly. Self-evaluation is key to unlocking the higher grades.

photo: Stewart Green

Self-Assessment Test

Score yourself between a one and a five on the following questions:

1. **I get anxious and tight as I head into crux sequences.**
   1—almost always, 2—often, 3—sometimes, 4—seldom, 5—never

2. **I miss "hidden" holds.**
   1—almost always, 2—often, 3—sometimes, 4—seldom, 5—never

3. **I have difficulty hanging on small, necessary-to-use holds.**
   1—almost always, 2—often, 3—sometimes, 4—seldom, 5—never

4. **I make excuses for why I might fail on a route before I even begin to climb.**
   1—almost always, 2—often, 3—sometimes, 4—seldom, 5—never

5. **My forearms "balloon" and my grip begins to fail even on routes that are "easy" for me.**
   1—almost always, 2—often, 3—sometimes, 4—seldom, 5—never

6. **On hard sequences, I have difficulty stepping onto critical footholds.**
   1—almost always, 2—often, 3—sometimes, 4—seldom, 5—never

7. **My footwork (use of feet) deteriorates during the hardest part of a climb.**
   1—almost always, 2—often, 3—sometimes, 4—seldom, 5—never

8. **I pump out on overhanging climbs no matter how big the holds.**
   1—almost always, 2—often, 3—sometimes, 4—seldom, 5—never

9. **I train or climb (or combination) three days in a row.**
   1—almost always, 2—often, 3—sometimes, 4—seldom, 5—never

10. **I grab quick draws, the rope, or other gear instead of risking a fall trying a hard move of which I am unsure.**
    1—almost always, 2—often, 3—sometimes, 4—seldom, 5—never

11. **I have difficulty reading sequences.**
    1—almost always, 2—often, 3—sometimes, 4—seldom, 5—never

12. **I experience elbow pain when I climb.**
    1—almost always, 2—often, 3—sometimes, 4—seldom, 5—never

13. **I have more difficulty climbing when people are watching.**
    1—almost always, 2—often, 3—sometimes, 4—seldom, 5—never

14. **My feet unexpectedly pop off foot holds.**
    1—almost always, 2—often, 3—sometimes, 4—seldom, 5—never

15. **I have difficult hanging onto small sloping holds or pockets.**
    1—almost always, 2—often, 3—sometimes, 4—seldom, 5—never

Calculate your score in the three focus areas.

Mental Questions	Technical Questions	Physical Questions
Q1: _____	Q2: _____	Q3: _____
Q4: _____	Q5: _____	Q6: _____
Q7: _____	Q8: _____	Q9: _____
Q10: _____	Q11: _____	Q12: _____
Q13: _____	Q14: _____	Q15: _____
Total: _____	Total: _____	Total: _____

Discussion, Tip and reference for each question

1. *Slow, deep breathing is the first step to reduce tension and anxiety.* TIP: Before starting a climb, close your eyes and take five deep breaths, each taking about 10 seconds. Try to maintain steady breathing as you climb. Take three more slow, deep breaths at each rest position and before the crux sequence. Learn the instant centering sequence for use at each rest position. (See Chapter 4.)

2. *Tunnel vision is a common cause of failure, especially during on-sight climbing.* TIP: Always completely scope a route before you leave the ground—view the route from a few different positions. As you climb, keep an open mind for hidden holds that may take a little extra effort to find. Chances are there is a good hand or foot hold escaping your view. (See Chapter 5.)

3. *Although poor body positioning can make small holds even harder to use, it is likely you need to increase your maximum grip strength.* TIP: Spend more time training on steep walls and gym "caves" areas, and go bouldering more often. Better yet, begin using hypergravity isolation training (HIT) as part of your training cycle. If a climbing wall is unavailable, I recommend some fingerboard training. (See Chapter 3.)

4. *Belief gives birth to reality. If thought of falling crosses your mind, you likely will.* TIP: Before you start up a climb, always visualize (vividly!) yourself successfully climbing the route from bottom to top. (See Chapter 4.)

5. *You are probably overgripping the holds and/or climbing too slowly.* TIP: On near-vertical walls relax your grip and place maximum weight on your feet. When the wall angle becomes overhanging, the number one rule is "climb fast!" (See Chapter 2.)

6. *Lack of flexibility is likely your problem.* TIP: Begin daily stretching for a minimum of 10 minutes. (See Chapter 3.)

7. *You may be focusing on the lack of good hand holds instead of zeroing in on crucial foot holds (often the key to unlocking hard sequences).* TIP: When the going gets tough renew focus on your feet. (See Chapters 2 and 5.)

8. *On overhanging walls the "pump clock" starts running when you leave the ground. You may not be too weak to climb the route, just too slow!* TIP: Practice climbing fast on known routes, and look for creative rests that will stop the clock for a few moments. (See Chapters 2 and 5.)

9. *This is a major error in training strategy that will eventually produce negative results because of overtraining and/or injury.* TIP: Never train three days in a row! Even the most conditioned climber should rarely climb on three consecutive days. (See Chapter 3.)

10. *Assuming the potential fall is safe, always go for the move instead of grabbing gear or hanging on the rope. The bad habit of grabbing gear is easy to develop and difficult to break. Plus, you'll never learn where your true limit is if you quit or cheat this way.* TIP: Counter any thought of grabbing gear with the vision of a good hold only one or two moves above you (there probably is!). (See Chapter 4.)

11. *Reading sequences comes from experience.* TIP: Climb up to four days a week. Do more on-sight climbing and always try to figure sequences from the ground before you attempt them for real. Put your visualization skills to work. (See Chapter 5.)

12. *There are two types on elbow tendinitis common to climbers. If you climb long enough, chances are you'll experience at least one of them.* TIP: Reverse wrist curls and hand pronators will help prevent these problems. Begin each workout with two sets of hand pronators and end each session with three sets of wrist curl (25 reps with a 5- to 15-pound dumbbell). (See Chapter 3.)

13. *Performing under unreasonable pressure is no fun, and the outcome is often less than ideal. The worst (and most common) pressure is the need to perform for others. This is unreasonable and must be shed.* TIP: Climb for yourself and forget the rest of the world. Relax, get centered, have fun! (See Chapter 4.)

14. *"Popping feet" is a common problem even among some advanced climbers. It can also result from too much indoor climbing (where the foot holds are more obvious).* TIP: Refocus your attention on your feet for a few weeks. Do you carefully place your feet on the best part of a hold or do you simply drop them onto the biggest-looking part? Also, do you hold your foot position stationary as you stand up on that leg? Start downclimbing routes to force your concentration down to your feet. (See Chapter 2.)

15. *Open-hand grip strength is crucial. Expert climbers favor it; beginner climbers avoid it.* TIP: Begin training and climbing with the open-hand grip. Try to do whole boulder problems, traverses or routes using only this grip. Employ HIT workouts to increase open-hand maximum strength most rapidly. (See Chapter 3.)

Rick Thompson on
"Access All Areas"
(5.11d), Northern West
Virginia.

Photo: Carl Samples

*Ian Spencer-Green on
"In Fear of Fear"
(5.13a), Elephant Rock,
Colorado.*

Photo: Stewart Green

Honing Your Skills—Fast!

If there is any secret at all (to the extraordinary success of French climbers), perhaps it is that we strive for grace, control and fluidity in movement.

—François Legrand

There are several elements to climbing skill including moves, body positions, tactics, and strategy. Since the playing field always changes, you need to become proficient at what seems to be thousands of variations on each of these elements. The range and complexity of motor learning in climbing is evident in the fact that an advanced climber with 20 years of experience can continue to learn new skills!

Your challenge is to maximize learning of climbing skills in every possible way. This immediately rules out the trial-and-error approach, which is just too slow if you are serious and passionate about this sport. Instead you need to embrace and aggressively utilize specific motor-learning techniques. In doing so you will ensure constant, noticeable improvements on the rock.

In this chapter I have outlined 16 such techniques and rules through which you can accelerate learning of climbing skill and maximize your ability. Understand them, believe in them, use them!

THE OPTIMAL AMOUNT OF CLIMB TIME

I'm frequently asked what is the ideal number of climbing days per week to maximize rate of improvement. Unfortunately, a single answer is impossible because it depends on many variables including skill level, type of climbing, strenuousness of the climbing workout, genetics, and quality of rest. Out of all these variables, the one that weighs most heavily is strenuousness of the climbing workout. There's a strong inverse relationship between the optimal amount of climbing days and the strenuousness of the climbing. Interestingly, this goes against conventional wisdom that says the stronger athlete performing more strenuous training can climb more. As usual, conventional wisdom is wrong!

Here's the scoop. A novice climber dedicated to learning the fundamental skills on non-strenuous terrain (for example, slab climbing or low-intensity vertical) can climb just about daily. As improvement takes place, the climber will begin work on steeper, longer and more strenuous routes. Due to the inverse relationship, such higher intensity climbing means

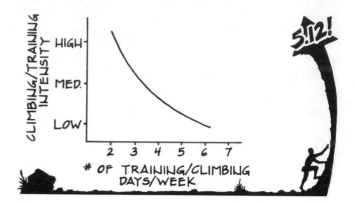

The more strenuous the workout or climbing the less frequently it should be performed.

fewer climbing days (and more rest days) are optimal. In this common scenario, two to four days a week of climbing is ideal.

The optimal length of a climbing workout is another difficult issue. The standard approach is to climb until completely fatigued. Research has shown this conventional approach is also flawed. Excessively long practice sessions of complex skills produce poor results, even for motor skills such as golf-range practice or shooting practice in basketball where physical fatigue is not a problem. Studies indicate it's best to keep actual practice time (in this case combined minutes of climbing) under two hours. In fact, half this amount seems to be optimal. About a dozen, five-minute routes in the gym seem like a good amount for practice of climbing skills.

Tip: Optimal, not maximal, practice produces the greatest gains in skill. Try for one hour of actual climbing time during each workout. Plan a total of three to five climbing and training days per week depending on the degree of strenuousness—the more strenuous the workout, the less frequently it should be done.

PRACTICE DAYS VERSUS PERFORMANCE DAYS

The difference between practice days and performance days lies in the desired outcome. Practice days are for maximal improvement of climbing skills with little concern for performance outcome. Performance days are simply about shredding routes and winning comps with no focus on learning or practicing specific climbing skills.

With the exception of elite climbers, practice days should rule. On these days you are free to work on new moves, experiment to find clever rest positions, and try new tactics and strategies, all without any concern or pressure not to fall. This curious and carefree approach will yield steady gains and an occasional major breakthrough!

Unfortunately, many climbers are plagued by the need to perform *all the time*. Not wanting to make a mistake and fall, they climb tentatively and are gun shy on trying chancy moves. Even worse, as insurance for good performances, they do the same routes, at the same areas or overdose on the local gym. The value of this approach is negligible.

Elite climbers are a different breed. With highly honed technical skills and fewer inhibitions, they generally don't hesitate on new moves and have little regard for the pressures of performance. In fact, performance days are their bread and butter. A heavy focus on outcome-based performance will train the few critical skills they may still be lacking: tactics, strategy, and the mental game. Plus, after years of hard work honing the zillions of basic skills, now's their time to bag some savage routes and win a big comp. Besides, nothing beats trial by fire for training elites in any sport.

Tip: Practice days have a greater training value than performance days for all but elite climbers. Each day you train or climb, predetermine whether the goal is practice or performance. Shoot for a 3 to 1 ratio of practice to performance time.

LEARNING NEW SKILLS

Your body learns and remembers new climbing movements by building detailed "motor performance maps" or schema in the nervous system and brain. New schema are best developed during the early portion of your workout while you are fresh to try unknown or difficult movements. Increasing fatigue, a flash pump, even fearful situations mean slow, maybe even no, learning of new climbing skills.

After a complete warmup, proceed straight into your skill training problems or routes— now's the time to add to your schema library! This may not be the most physical part of your session, but it can be the most productive if it's heavily focused on new or problem techniques, moves, or situations. Whether it's delicate face climbing, drop knees on overhanging rock or thin handcrack technique, jump on it fresh.

A safe, fear-free environment is also a big help at learning new moves fast. Indoor walls win the prize here because of convenience and comfort. But get outside as much as possible because no gym can match the variety of moves available on real rock. Either way, start off working your most uncomfortable skills or type of terrain while you're fresh.

Tip: Practice of new skills is most effective when you're well rested, fully warmed up, and in a safe environment. Use the 30 minutes immediately following your warm up to practice new moves, techniques, and weak skills areas. Indoor walls, topropes, and boulders are the ideal forum.

Top rope climbing is a great way to learn new moves or practice difficult sequences. Here the powerful Doug Reed pulls through a burley roof sequence.

Photo: Carl Samples

BLOCKED PRACTICE OF DIFFICULT MOVES

"Blocked" practice (identical repetitions of a move) is the most popular method of training hard climbing skills whether at the gym or crag. However, misuse of blocked practice is common among climbers and can have negative effects on performance. Let's sort things out.

Blocked, repetitive practice of new skills will produce rapid positive results. For instance, when learning a difficult boulder problem, you perform repeated attempts of the exact desired sequence. Or suppose you want to learn finger-jamming technique, the focus is laps on fingercracks for a session or two. These are both appropriate uses of blocked practice.

Upon development of "feel" and confidence and some rate of success at the new task, a radical change is needed. Further blocked reps have little value and may even result in a false sense of confidence and poor use of the skill in settings different from that practiced. An example would be a climber who has wired a route at his or her home crag through countless ascents but can't send similar routes on a road trip. The same phenomena is seen in other sports, like a golfer who hits perfectly during regular practices at the range (blocked) but is in the trees, sand, and water during rare visits to a course.

These examples show that beyond the first few successful trials of a task, blocked practice is for block heads! Beyond this point, additional gains require variable and randomization of practice.

Tip: Use blocked practice to accelerate learning during the initial trials of a new move, skill, or sequence. After two or three successful repititions, cease blocked practice in favor of variable and randomized practice.

VARIABLE PRACTICE OF SKILLS

It's not enough to acquire use of a move or skill in a single setting. The ultimate goal is instant and proficient use of the skill in any novel situation you come upon. The tried and proven way to do this is with variable practice.

Climber A has developed more diverse schema (dots) and thus will be able to closely approximate the novel move (★), possibly onsight it!

Climber B's more limited schema will have him flailing and probably failing on the novel move (★).

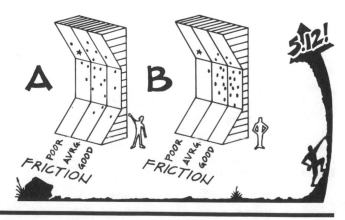

Suppose you've just learned the drop-knee move on a vertical indoor wall with large, positive holds. To incorporate variable practice you would now change the "route" conditions slightly and attempt the same drop-knee move again. After a few reps in this situation change the conditions even more.

Indoor walls are ideal for variable practice sessions. Do the desired move one way, then change the hold size and try it again. Adjust the spacing of the holds and attempt another rep. Finally, switch to another section of wall and perform the move at a different angle. Change the conditions every few trials whether you succeed or not, to prevent blocking of the practice.

Now the exciting part: Variable practice of a move over several workouts will develop solid schema relating to use of the move over a wide range of conditions (angle, hold size, rock type, and friction properties). Such schema enable you to perform moves in novel situations on-sight, even if you've never done that exact move in practice! Elite climbers often comment after sending a route on-sight that the right moves

Variable practice of moves develops solid schema. Here the back-step is practiced in six increasingly difficult situations (left to right)

...ial leaning of the ...ckstep move in an ...y vertical setting.

The same move is practiced on a slightly overhanging wall.

Further practice on smaller holds on a slightly overhanging wall

...ckstep move practiced ...a steeper wall with ...ge holds.

A more difficult backstep move with tiny footholds, and a small undercling hand hold.

Backsteps on severely overhanging walls are most difficult to learn, but most valuable to add to your schema library!

and body positions "came to them intuitively." They have their schema to thank for the success.

Tip: Variable practice expands the learning of newly acquired skills for use over a wide range of conditions (angle, hold size, rock type, and so forth). Use this drill regularly, always varying the "route" conditions greater than you expect they'll ever occur on a route. Change the conditions every few attempts to avoid blocked practice.

SKILL GUIDANCE METHODS

The main methods of skill guidance in climbing are verbal help in solving a sequence and physical aid in executing a move. Although both are effective in facilitating learning, misuse can produce long-term negative effects. Verbal description of moves and sequences is invaluable during early stages of learning. Such spoon-feed instruction accelerates learning by short-cutting the slower trial-and-error approach. This is completely appropriate for a novice climber.

Unfortunately, excessive "beta" (as it's commonly called) beyond the earliest stages of learning can interfere with the development of problem-solving skills, inhibit learning of complex movements, and ultimately degrade your future climbing potential. Research clearly shows that even moderate amounts of verbal guidance yield poor performances when the guidance is removed. Thus, if your goal is simply to get up a route (redpoint) as fast as possible, maximum verbal guidance will aid your performance. However, if your long-term goal is a broad proficiency in this sport with maximum on-sight and competitive skills, beta is a handicap that will hold you back.

Physical guidance aids learning of difficult or strenuous moves.

A good spotter both protects against dangerous falls and is ready to lend some physical aid when learning a difficult move.

The second type of guidance is physical help through a move, via a yank on the rope, or a push on the bum. Once again, such guidance is an excellent aid in learning a new skill when used sparingly. Physical aids are best used in bouldering where just a light touch is enough to coax you through a move. More invasive physical aids such as getting hauled through a sequence by your belayer or pushed into an awkward position by your spotter have minimal benefits.

Tip: Use skill guidance to accelerate learning of moves and sequences. Ask (demand) verbal and physical aid when attempting a new skill or in search of a quick ascent. However, avoid excessive skill guidance (especially beta) as it will produce long-term negative results. Don't hesitate to "shout off" beta and figure out the move yourself!

SELF-AWARENESS OF PERFORMANCE

Keen self-awareness is crucial for optimal climbing performance. In context of this chapter, your task is to monitor your climbing technique and efficiency of movement. Ultimately, it's the aggregate of minor inefficiencies and slight flaws in technique that bring a climber down short of reaching the summit. The evidence is played out at gyms and crags across the country. We've all seen and experienced it. It goes like this.

A group of climbers are working a route whose crux sequence has one best solution. Each climber attempts the same sequence, but only one person succeeds. Why does the sequence work for one person but not the others? In many cases the answer lies in a number of minor technical flaws which are unknowing sabotaging performances. These flaws may range from climbing too slowly, to undue tension in antagonistic muscles, to sloppy placements of the feet, to overgripping of holds, to mental miscues. The key to nixing these problems is self-awareness—never-ending checks and rechecks of the goings on in your mind and body, followed by tiny adjustments. Elite climbers probably do this hundreds of times during a single ascent (often unknowingly!). Beginners, on the other hand, may never do it because they are overwhelmed by the immediate concern of solving the next move.

Make a conscious effort to develop this skill early on in your climbing career. It will enhance your performance and help in identification and elimination of bad habits. Remember, just as climbing skills become "hard wired" after a few repetitions, so do bad habits such as overgripping and sloppy feet.

Tip: Constant self-awareness is essential for improving poor skills, eliminating bad habits, and increasing performance quality. Ask yourself questions to increase this awareness. For example, is this the best body position? Am I using proper footwork and minimal upper body strength? Am I climbing at the best pace?

MODELING ADVANCED CLIMBERS

One type of guidance you can never overdose on is modeling of advanced climbers. Whether in business or sports, modeling someone successful is one of the surest ways to find out what works.

Modeling is best used in a climbing gym where you can observe the movements, positions, and techniques of advanced climbers, then give them a try on your own. Make a mental picture of what you want to attempt and use that vision as a starting point. Experiment, modify, and make the move your own. Who knows, you just might find a better way of doing it!

You can also model what you observe at the crags. In addition to actual moves, take special note of the tactics and strategy used by high-end climbers. For example, how do they

Modeling advanced climbers' technique, tactics and movements is a great method of learning.

Here Bobbi Bensman executes a great clipping position—straight arm with weight in over the feet—you can model.

Photo: Stewart Green

"work" crux sequences? Where do they find rests? At what pace do they climb? How do they go about equipping routes? Again, it's best to first experiment with your observations in the gym before you test them outdoors.

Although modeling technical skills is a powerful weapon for your arsenal, copying an elite climber's fitness training can easily backfire. Remember, elite climbers have spent years conditioning their muscles and tendons to withstand extreme levels of stress. To train as they do without this long-term preparation could be disastrous.

Tip: Modeling the techniques and tactics (not training) of advanced climbers is a powerful learning tool. Begin to spend as much time observing other climbers as you do actually climbing. Take note of new moves, rest positions, tactics, and such, and experiment with them on your own. The images you pick up are the seeds to future advancements.

DEVELOPING A BROAD REPERTOIRE OF SKILLS

One of the oldest principles in the field of motor learning and performance is that "transfer of learning between two tasks increases as the similarity between them increases." This explains why proficiency in one type of climbing does not guarantee success in any other. We've all seen climbers who excel in just one style (for example, traditional) or at one angle (for example, steep sport routes), or even one area; however, it's quite rare to find a person who's brilliant across the board. Here's why.

Suppose you spend most of your time climbing artificial walls. You'll certainly get good at climbing said terrain, but venture outdoors and you'll be in for a good spanking. Or what if you specialize in crack climbing? Although you may become a stonemaster of Valley cracks, an attempt on a Rifle sport route would have the fat lady singing by the second bolt.

Michael Jordan proved that basketball-throwing skills do not transfer well to baseball-throwing skills. So don't expect indoor climbing skills to transfer outdoors or for face climbing skills to transfer to cracks. To become a great climber you need to log extensive wide-ranging practice. Real rock is the ticket here, and the more you travel to different areas the better. You'll develop a broad set of schema and ultimately perform well in any situation.

Travel to as wide a variety of areas as possible. Limiting your experiences means limiting your ability.
Kyle Hörst is pictured here on a classic traditional route at Seneca Rocks, West Virginia.

Thus, although specializing in one type of climbing (say sport climbing) will yield the most rapid short-term gains, such blocked practice will limit your potential in all other areas. Conversely, long-term exposure to many types of climbing can enhance performance in your specialty area. For instance, sport climbers can use crack techniques like hand and knee jambs for a vital rest—that is, if they know the technique!

Tip: Climbing on a wide variety of rock is the single most important element of skill training. Get outdoors and travel as much as possible to develop a wide repertoire of techniques, tactics, and moves. Avoid specialization since it will limit your long-term potential.

ON-SIGHT PRACTICE PAYOFFS

Climbing is a complex game of problem solving, strategy, movement, and mental fortitude. You will never realize your true potential unless you work consistently on all these areas. On-sight climbing is the most powerful means of developing these skills in proportion to one another.

On-sighting is defined as climbing with zero prior knowledge, information, or clues of any kind. Thus on-sighting a chalked sport route or tagged indoor climb is a somewhat

Mike Freeman has on-sighted hundreds of routes at the Gunks. Here he is cranking at the Millbrook cliff.

Photo: Michael Miller

dilute form of on-sight. This fine point aside, heading up on any kind of climb with the burden of deciphering it yourself holds great practice value. The purer the on-sight, the greater the value, of course.

As discussed earlier, verbal guidance (beta) is only useful in the formative stages of learning. To the intermediate or advanced climber, beta yields only short-term gratification with no long-term benefits. It's as if Bobby Fisher spoon-fed every move to you during a chess match you were playing. You'd surely win the match but gain no skill as his pawn (pun intended).

Tip: On-sight climbing develops the widest range of technical and cognitive skills. Climb on-sight weekly, whether at the gym or crags. It's like taking skill-building steroids—but these side effects are good for you!

THE SYNERGY OF MENTAL AND PHYSICAL PRACTICE

Interlacing mental and physical practice undoubtedly yields faster learning of sport skills than either alone. If you are not employing mental practice between every climbing rep and during rest days, you are surely giving up a major edge. Use of mental imagery can range from simply visualizing a move before you try it to running a detailed mental movie of a long, sequential climb prior to a redpoint. Repeat the visualization often making the images as accurate, detailed, and vivid as possible. This will provide best results.

As with physical skills, your mental abilities will improve with practice. Always "climb" each sequence or route at least once mentally before attempting it. Sure, it takes extra effort and time to exercise your imagination in this way, but the payoffs are very real! It's a safe bet that not a single Olympic athlete gives away this powerful edge, so why should you?

Tip: Interlacing mental and physical practice of skills produces greater results than physical practice alone. Visualize a new move or sequence at least once before each attempt to enhance learning and increase the odds of success. Employ regular mental practice during rest periods (or days) to build confidence and further "code" known sequences.

SPEED TRAINING OF SKILLS

One of the most ignored yet important climbing skills is climbing fast. No, not speed climbing as in the competitions, but faster-than-normal movement through hard sequences without loss of technique. This is fundamental for conserving energy on difficult routes, but it takes practice.

Known or "wired" routes at the gym or local crag are ideal to begin training this skill. Since you already know the moves, you can move briskly through difficult sections with little thought. Concentrate on climbing quickly from one rest position to the next. Your goal is not to race to the top with sloppy, inefficient moves, but instead to climb as fast as possible while maintaining perfect technique. Slow down at the first sign you're making errors, whether it's a foot pop or botched sequence. Climbing fast in poor form has no value.

You may want to occasionally experiment with accelerated on-sight climbing since most climbers tend to climb too slowly in this setting. Pick a lengthy toprope climb at the gym or a well-bolted sport climb so safety is not a concern. Scope the route extensively and visualize as many of the moves as you can from the ground. When you are relaxed and ready, attack the route with a vengeance and don't worry about the outcome. Remember, this is practice.

After a few months, you will find yourself climbing faster on all routes, on-sight or not. This drill will clear up your misconceptions about the "right" speed to climb on different types of routes. Your efficacy will skyrocket thanks to heightened awareness of the relationship between speed and fatigue.

Tip: Performing known sequences and routes at accelerated speed increases long-term proficiency. Use "speed climbing" at least once a week to stretch the bonds of where you can climb both quickly and accurately.

DOWNCLIMBING ROUTES

Every time you lower off the top of a climb you miss out on one of the most effective training exercises: downclimbing. That's right, if you really want to get better in this sport, and fast, then rechalk at the top of a route and begin climbing back down.

Downclimbing improves many skills including footwork, sense of body positioning, speed of movement, hold recognition, and sequence memory to name a few. It's also great fitness training since you're increasing the length of your "burn" and performing eccentric muscle movements. All totaled, this makes downclimbing a hands-down must on all but performance days.

Clearly, toprope setups facilitate more carefree, go-for-it attempts at downclimbing a route. Whether at the gym or a crag find a good belayer who can pay out rope at just the right rate—you don't want to get hung up by the rope while reversing the crux sequence! Continue downclimbing until muscular failure or you botch a sequence and fall. Whether you get back on and continue or lower to the ground (on a steep route you may have no choice) is up to you. Do be careful not to go overboard on this training method. If you fall more than a few times downclimbing, call it quits and move on to the next (up) climb.

I cautiously advise downclimbing of lead routes. Overhanging sport routes are the best choice here; in fact, downclimbing is a nice alternative to untying and threading anchors. However, a veteran belayer is mandatory, especially as you enter the ground-out zone near the last (lower) two bolts.

Tip: Downclimbing routes is a powerful skill-training exercise. Don't overlook this method of training the triad of skill, fitness, and mental abilities. On practice days, downclimb (as far as possible) every route you send.

FATIGUED SKILL PRACTICE

Earlier I pointed out it's best to practice new skills while you're fresh. Interestingly, you can increase your command of known skills through practice during states of moderate fatigue. This is a powerful concept you'll want to put to work immediately but be careful not to misuse it.

Research has shown that beyond the initial successful trials of a skill, practice should be performed with variable conditions and levels of fatigue. This will increase your rate of failure at doing certain moves, but performance isn't your goal, practice is! The benefits of this practice, no matter how poor, will become evident in the future. Besides, this concept actually makes good sense. If you want the ability to stick a deadpoint in the midst of a dicey lead climb while pumped, you'd better log some deadpoints in various states of fatigue during practice.

Here's the best approach. Use the first 30 minutes of your

workout (while fresh) to train new skills, then move on to chalking up some mileage on a variety of routes. After an hour or so, or when moderately fatigued, attempt several reps of recently acquired moves or sequences. As fatigue increases, finish up with some reps of sequences or boulder problems you have more completely mastered.

In the context of a two-hour climbing gym workout, this rule emphasizes the benefit of squeezing in a greater volume of climbing with only brief rests, over doing just a few "performance" reps with extensive rest. The long rests and performance climbing may make you look better, but the greater volume of practice will make you climb better!

Finally, don't confuse practice while muscularly fatigued with practice while tired or injured. As with any training method, you can go overboard and end up getting negative results. Sixty to ninety minutes of actual climbing time is optimal.

Tip: Practice recently acquired skills while moderately fatigued to increase your mastery of them and to build long-term retention. Attempting well-known skills and sequences during higher levels of fatigue is likewise beneficial.

RANDOM SKILL PRACTICE

The ability to on-sight a sequence of novel moves on "foreign" rock is the ultimate goal of your skill practice time. To this end, the best workout approach (after practicing new skills while fresh) is a randomized free-for-all of skill types. This highly effective method is widely used in other sports and should not be overlooked by climbers as top training for the "unknown."

There are two approaches to random training of climbing skills. First, on an indoor wall attempt to link a sequence of very different bouldering moves. Put your right brain to work on contriving a bizarre (not hard) random sequence of moves. Take several tries at sending it. Better yet, team up with your most deranged friend on a round of the "stick game" (a.k.a. "send me"). Take turns pointing (with a broomstick) each other through a perverse sequence of movements. The ideal route is an unlikely, random selection of moderately difficult moves.

The second, more powerful method of randomization training is to climb a series of widely differing routes in rapid succession. A commercial gym with many different angles, a few cracks, and a roof or two is ideal. Team with a partner and toprope 5 to 10 routes of different character within an hour. The first route may be a vertical face, the next a slab, the third a fingercrack, the fourth an overhanging pumpfest, the fifth a handcrack, the sixth a roof route, etc. This rapid recall of a wide range of techniques is skill training at its best.

"Send Me" is an excellent method of Random Skill Practice.

You can use both of these random practice methods outdoors as well. The advantage of real rock is a wider range of route and move types, with the downside of it taking longer to locate and setup appropriate routes.

Tip: Random practice of known skills enhances functional use and long-term recall. Do a random-skill workout at least once a week. Use as wide a range of moves and route types as possible to maximize effectiveness.

FEEDBACK AND VIDEO ANALYSIS

The best climbers seem to have no obvious "weak areas." They perform well in just about any setting, any time. This is largely due to their understanding and use of many of the aforementioned skill-training methods. However, it's their relentless pursuit of identifying and fixing weak areas, with the goal of perfection, that separates the best from the rest.

It begins with day-to-day self-awareness and self-analysis of every aspect of your practice and performance. But it can't stop there; some problems require an objective point of view to be fully revealed. For starters, an instructor, coach, or even your partner can provide verbal feedback and guidance as you climb. Their guidance should be focused on pointing out poor technique or tactics not on giving beta.

Another popular method of feedback in sports is videotape. Have a friend (not your belayer) videotape you climbing several different types of routes. If possible get some footage both indoors and out and on toprope and lead. View the tape straight through, noting differences in your style, control, attack and emotions from one route type to the next and between toprope and lead. This evaluation alone should provide tons of feedback on your general strengths and weaknesses.

Next, dissect each climb in detail with liberal use of rewind and slow-motion play. Take note of even the most minor "problems" whether bent arms in a rest position, scraping feet in the midst of a crux, tight slow movements, lack of decisiveness and go for it, or whatever.

After reviewing a route on tape and noting errors, visualize the desired corrections to each problem. Make a mental movie with all the right moves spliced in place of the outtakes. When feasible, return to the climb and attempt the corrections you've envisioned.

The power of videotape in enhancing performance cannot be overstated. All types of performers from network newscasters to professional football players spend hours each week reviewing footage in search of even the smallest glitch in performance. I challenge you to commit a minimum of two hours per month to video analysis. It's invaluable, and it's a blast!

Tip: Get frequent feedback from your partner, a coach, or more advanced climber. Better yet, use video analysis to critique yourself and identify your weaknesses du jour. Make written notes of what you observe, then use visualization to build a blueprint of an alternate, correct reality you'll execute on the rock.

The author on-sighting 5.12 in the Frankenjura, Germany.

Photo: Mike McGill

Mia Axon on "Missing Link" (5.12b/c), Bear Canyon, Boulder, Colorado.

Photo: Stewart Green

Welcome to Conditioning

*The hardest part of training is making the
decision to start at all.*
                    —Wolfgang Güllich

The desire for greater strength is inherent in most athletes—climbers are no exception. Increased strength is
handy as you crank increasingly hideous routes on your trip
toward 5.12 (and, of course, beyond). Getting honed and
buffed also helps the "head games," as more strength breeds
confidence and greater confidence breeds success.

Unfortunately, too many climbers obsess on strength training prior to perfecting the fundamentals of climbing movement. This approach will stunt technical growth, mushroom
frustrations, and all but zero the chances of attaining the skill
and strength to become a true master of rock. So whether
your long-term goal is an invitation to Todd Skinner's winter
training camp, a call to train with the seriously strong Franklin
Climbing design team (Yaniro, Pont, Cronin, and Scotty), or
just to climb 5.10 someday, exercise your patience and put first
things first. Dialing in technique and tactics must be the top
priority, while maximizing strength is far in second place.

This chapter provides a streamlined three-part discussion
on getting fit for the rocks. Let's begin by examining the
essential issues of physical conditioning for beginner- to intermediate-level climbers. Next is a cutting-edge, to-the-point
look into sport-specific strength training for more advanced
climbers. The chapter concludes with details on preventing
injury and speeding recovery from severe workouts through
proper nutrition and rest.

Keep in mind that this chapter is *not* a comprehensive text
on strength training. Consult *Flash Training* for a broader discussion of this topic, and remember there is always more to
come in the future!

GENERAL FITNESS CONDITIONING

Physical fitness is one of the three factors in the "climbing
performance equation," the others being your technical and
mental abilities. While climbing will yield positive results in
all three areas, pure fitness training will only make you more
fit. Thus, as Absolute #3 (Chapter 1) points out, most persons
will cash in a greater return in performance from time invested climbing than in fitness training.

What about beginner- to intermediate-level climbers who
still want or need to do some fitness training? They should

The author high over the Verdon in southern France.

Photo: Mike McGill

focus on four areas: reducing body weight, increasing flexibility, general muscular conditioning, and improving strength in the "pull muscles."

Lose the Fat, Thin the Muscle

If you've ever climbed with a big pack, heavy rack, or a long, thick rope, you've experienced the negative affects of increased weight on performance. Likewise, reasonable weight loss can have a strong positive affect. Your goal is not the anorexic supermodel look, but instead a tight "V-shaped" physique featuring the skinny legs of a long-distance runner and an upper body somewhat like a gymnast.

First, let's state the obvious. Excessive body fat is bad. But so is excessively low body fat, which will leave you weak, slow to recover, and unable to build muscle. The optimal body fat percentage for men is 6 to 12 percent and 8 to 16 percent for women. If you're not sure how you measure up, consider having your body fat tested. Or you can use the economic "pinch-an-inch" method on your waistline (actually a good gauge). If you can pinch an inch, you are *not* in the optimal ranges.

For a climber, excessive muscular weight is about as bad as excessive fat. In fact, since muscle weighs more than fat per unit volume, large muscles in the wrong place are worse than fat. As a comparison, imagine Arnold Schwarzenegger and Rush Limbaugh sieging a route at Smith Rocks. The results would be hugely negative for both men!

Inappropriate training is the usual cause of unwanted muscle. For instance, the leg exercises performed by bodybuilders or bike racers are a waste of time for climbers since lack of leg strength is rarely the limiting factor on the rock. Biceps curls and heavy bench- and shoulder-press exercises are another example. They will pump you up nicely for the beach but weigh you down on the rock. What is your priority?

There are two common methods of stripping away unwanted fat and muscle that have worked for climbers. First, is the low-fat, low-protein, low-calorie diet combined with maximum climbing (a popular method for on-the-road climbers trying to live on a dollar a day). Although initial results may be positive, the long-term effects of consistent undernutrition (lack of calories and protein) is a plateau (or drop) in performance, excessive loss of muscle, sickness, and/or injury.

A better approach for reaching optimal body weight is a high-quality (not high-calorie) diet and regular aerobic activity. The diet should consist of "three squares," with a total caloric breakdown of approximately 65 percent carbohydrate, 20 percent protein, and 15 percent fat. Activity-wise, running is

General Fitness Conditioning Tips:

• Reducing body weight is often the fastest way to increase strength-to-weight ratio. If you are overweight (or overly muscular), make aerobic training and a high-quality diet a priority. Remember, weight loss will yield faster gains in apparent strength than actual strength training. Run up to 30 minutes three to seven days per week. Taper the amount of aerobic activity as you approach optimal body weight.

• Flexibility training aids development of some technical skills and lowers potential for injury. Stretch before and after every workout for at least 5 to 15 minutes to enable unhindered movement and speed muscular recovery, respectively.

• Climbing is the best general strength training for climbing. If you climb at least three days per week, there is little need for supplemental strength training during your formative years. Vary the type of climbing to maximize the all-around fitness training effect.

• Keep supplemental training specific to climbing. Buy a fingerboard or pull-up bar or, better yet, build a home wall. Favor body-weight exercises over machines and keep the resistance low.

most effective for incinerating fat and shrinking unwanted muscle. Don't worry about your "climbing muscles;" they will be maintained as long as you continue to climb regularly and consume at least 1 gram of protein per kilogram of body weight per day. Other popular aerobic activities such as heavy-duty biking and the StairMaster yield mixed results as they do eat up body fat but may maintain (or build) undesirable leg muscle.

Frequency of aerobic training should be proportional to your distance from ideal weight. For example, if you are far overweight, then daily 20- to 30-minute runs are an important part of your training-for-climbing program. As you near ideal weight, one to three 20-minute runs per week are sufficient. Upon reaching your optimal weight, little or no aerobic training is required since cragging requires only modest aerobic fitness. Your training time is better invested on sport-specific exercises or climbing.

Flexibility Training

Okay, I admit it. I hate stretching! After all, it's human nature to hate doing things at which we're poor and my flexibility stinks. Seriously, athletes can't ignore any weaknesses if they want to continue to improve. I have developed the habit of stretching before and after each workout, and I've made some modest improvements to boot. Of course, I real-

SIX KEY STRETCHES

1. Froggies (a.k.a. butterflies). This stretch works the "hip turnout" so crucial for climbing near-vertical walls. Lie flat on your back, places the soles of your feet together with your legs bent about three-quarters of the way. Relax and allow your knees to drop to the side toward the floor. You can increase the stretch by having someone carefully apply pressure onto your knees. Perform five stretches each lasting 20 to 30 seconds.

2. Wall splits. This is an easy stretch for the groin and legs. Start with your legs elevated and together, with your butt a few inches away from the wall. Slowly separate your legs (heels resting on the wall) until you feel the stretch begin. Keep your lower back to the floor throughout and let gravity pull your legs out (down) to the side. Hold the stretch for two to four minutes.

3. High steps. This "active" stretch is the best single exercise to improve the valuable high-step skill. Stand against an unused section of vertical climbing wall with your feet forward and toes touching the wall. Grab two hand holds for balance and lift one leg as high as possible to your side as if to step on a hold at hip level (if there's actually a hold there then place your foot on it!). Repeat this high-step stretch 10 times on both sides. Try to step a bit higher each time without moving away from the wall.

4. Forearm stretch. Mandatory! While standing, place the fingers of the straight arm (arm to be stretched) into the palm of the opposite hand. Pull back on the fingers/hand of the straight arm until you feel the stretch begin. Hold for 10 seconds. Now flex the hand in the other direction and pull gently to stretch the back of the forearm. Do three, 10-second stretches of each forearm.

ize I'll never be doing disco splits like Tim "TNT" Toula. Flexibility is largely determined by genetics, so the goal is to stretch enough to realize my potential. In doing so, I open up more moves on vertical face climbs, lower the chance of certain injuries, and speed recovery after workouts.

Whether you are gifted in this area or not, there are six basic stretches I consider the minimum requirements. Do them before and after each workout. Consider them mandatory at the start of a day at the crags.

5. Shoulder and upper back. Pull your elbow across your chest toward the opposite shoulder. While still pulling, slowly move the elbow up and down to work the complete stretch.

6. Upper arm and lat. With arms overhead and bent at the elbows, grab one elbow and pull it behind your head until you feel a stretch in the triceps and shoulder. Finish by slowing leaning sideways in the direction of the stretch to extend it below the shoulder and into the lat muscles. As with previous stretches remember to work both sides.

Tip: Perform a few minutes of light aerobic activity (for example, jogging or jumping rope) before beginning your stretching. After stretching, massage your fingers, hands, and forearms for a few minutes. This increases warming blood flow to the connective tissues, tendons, and muscles most stressed while climbing.

Strength Training 101 (or Intro to Strength Training)

The importance of muscular strength to climbing performance has probably been obvious since your first pump on the first climb of your first day on the rock. The natural conclusion is to place a high priority on gaining more strength in the forearms, upper arms, and back. Unfortunately, this is the biggest and most common error in training for climbing. An obsession on strength training early on will stunt your technical growth and may handicap your climbing skill for years to come.

Absolute #3 (see Chapter 1) emphasized that gains in performance come more quickly from practice of climbing skills than strength training during the formative years. The good news is that in addition to increasing skill, climbing is also a pretty good muscular workout. It's the two-birds-with-one-stone idea: Climb as a workout and you'll improve both skill and strength. If you go to the health club for a strength workout, you will gain some strength (although it may not be specific to climbing) but you will do nothing to develop skill.

Climbing long routes or lapping short ones trains muscular endurance. Working on crux moves and general bouldering will help build strength. Get on a variety of terrain and literally every muscle from your feet to your forearms will get into the act. Muscular workouts like this are far more useful than doing a circuit of machines at the local health club. Forget the iron. Get climbing!

SUPPLEMENTAL EXERCISES

Pull-Muscle Exercises

1. Pull-ups. This most obvious exercise for climbers is useful for beginners but hardly worth the time for elites. Use a large hold on a fingerboard or a pull-up bar with palms away grip. Do five sets to failure with a two- to three-minute rest between sets. Three days per week is optimal.

Your long-term goal is five sets of 15 repetitions. When you reach this begin to add weight around your waist (that is ballast not fat!). If to start you can't do five sets of at least eight reps (not to worry, it's common) have a spotter help you achieve as many as it takes to reach eight. Or use a chair to step up to the top position and lower to a 10-second count. Either way, you must always achieve a minimum of eight reps!

2. Uneven grip pull-ups. Put your hand on the bar, the other between 6 and 18 inches lower, holding on to a towel looped over the bar (or with two or three fingers through a loop of webbing). Both hands pull, with the upper hand emphasized. Do a set to failure, then rest a minute and switch sides. Repeat twice. Increase the vertical distance between hands if you can do eight or more reps. Do this twice a week and in a few months to a year you'll be close to doing a one-arm pull-up!

3. Lat pull-down. Do this in place of, not in addition to, pull-ups. This is one exercise you can do like the bodybuilders, although your hand spacing should vary only a few inches from shoulder width (if you don't perform uneven grip pull-ups, then you would benefit from working the lat pull-downs one arm at a time). Use a heavy weight that allows you just 6 to 12 high-intensity reps. Take a two-

minute rest between five total sets. Do these a maximum of two days per week.

Supplemental Strength-Training Exercises

Some supplemental strength training is advised if you can't climb three or four days per week. Your workout must be tailored to climbing—a friend's bodybuilding workout won't do. Put some thought into figuring out what exercises are most specific to climbing. The closer the exercise is to the actual climbing positions the better. For instance, pull-ups are similar to more climbing movements than, say, biceps curls. Fingerboard hangs are specific to how you grip the rock;

4. Frenchies. These babies will fry your pull muscles. Do three sets one day per week in addition to other pull-muscle exercises. Start at the top position of a pull-up (palms away, hands shoulder width apart) and hold there in a lock-off position for seven seconds. Lower to the bottom and pull-up to the top again; however, this time immediately lower half way (arm angle of 90 degrees) and hold a lock-off there for seven seconds. Lower to the bottom and do another pull-up after which you'll lock-off at an arm angle of about 120 degrees. Hold for seven seconds and lower to the bottom position. Perform this exact sequence and you've done one full cycle—but keep going if you can! Do as many continuous cycles, or part there of, until failure. Rest five minutes between sets. Don't cheat on the seven-second counts!

5. Fingerboard hangs "Repeaters" may be the single best fingerboard regimen as they will build contact strength in a variety of grips. One set of repeaters involves a series of six, maximum-intensity hangs (on the same hold) lasting 3 to 10 seconds each and separated by just a five-second rest. Favor small- to medium-sized edges, pockets and pinches. Do two consecutive sets on each of six to ten different grips (12 to 20 total sets). Each set must be maximum intensity, so add weight to your body to ensure failure in 10 seconds on each rep. Rest one minute between sets. Always perform a good warmup including a few easy hangs on the holds to be worked. Limit yourself to two repeater workouts per week.

hand-held squeezers are not. A lat pulldown machine at the gym is somewhat specific to climbing; the bench press is not. If you're not sure about an exercise, nix it. And most of all, ignore what the muscleheads are doing.

In addition, favor body-weight exercises such as push-ups and dips over machines or free weights. If you possess ordinary leg strength (for example, you are able to step up stairs two or three at a time), forget any strength training for the legs. Keep the weights light (between 50 and 75 percent of body weight) when using free weights and machines. The

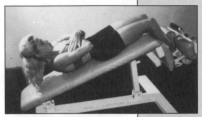

6. Abdominal crunches. These can be done on the floor with your feet and lower legs up on a chair and knees bent at 90 degrees or on a decline bench. Cross your arms over your chest and lift your shoulders off the floor or bench. Exhale with each "up" repetition and continue until failure. One minute rest between three to five sets is plenty.

As you progress onto harder and steeper routes, add some Hanging Leg Raises to your ab workout. Hang from a pull-up bar and lift your knees toward your chest. Three sets to failure will hit your abs better than a lifetime of using the Ab Flex™, Ab Roller™ or any of that other junk.

7. Reverse wrist curls. Using a 10- or 15-pound dumbbell, perform these wrist curls palm down and with your forearm resting on your knee, a bench, or table for support. Do approximately 20 half repetitions; that is, begin with your hand in the neutral position (straight), then curl it up and back until it's fully extended.

8. Hand pronators. Exercise machines and devices for working hand pronation are a rarity—if you find one, buy it. Otherwise, you can whip up a makeshift pronation trainer in a few minutes. Cut a 12-inch piece of broom stick and mount just a few 1-pound weights securely on one end (actually 1.25-pound York barbell weights are ideal and can be purchased at most sporting goods stores). Hold the free end in the hand to be trained. Vary resistance either by adding weight or moving your hand farther down the stick (away from the weighted end).

Hand Pronators can be done sitting or standing with your arm bent at 90 degrees and your elbow propped against your leg (sitting) or your waist (standing). Two to three sets of 20 repetitions are ideal before each workout.

exceptions are pulldown exercises, which you can work at body weight or higher. High resistances build muscle and the "pullers" are the only place this is acceptable.

ADVANCED FITNESS CONDITIONING

If you've been climbing a few years, can send 5.10 in your sleep, and your technique and tactical skills are up to snuff, you are ready to embark on some serious sport-specific strength training. Still, you must not obsess on this aspect of training at the expense of everything else. Jump into this type of training too early or too fast and it will hurt your technical growth and get you injured. Proceed with caution and remember this section is just a primer on the subject and certainly *not* the final word.

John Cronin climbing in the Coliseum at Summerville Lake, West Virginia.

Photo: Michael Miller

Sport-Specific Strength Training

Advanced fitness conditioning for climbing is all about the pull muscles. You might take it one step further and say it's all about finger strength. To meet this need, numerous exercises and protocols have been publicized over the years. Everything from fingertip pulls to fingerboards to massive bouldering to various squeeze devices have been used with mixed results. Ultimately, the usefulness of these exercises depends on a number of things, including their ability to bring about rapid muscular failure and their specificity to finger use while climbing. Let's try to sort things out.

The most specific type of finger training is obviously climbing itself. I strongly advise every serious climber to join a commercial gym or build a home wall. Although indoor walls are a poor simulator of outdoor climbing, they are most efficient at providing a sport-specific pump.

Home gyms are key! Just you and some friends climbing, with no hustle or hassles of commercial gyms. And it's always open. For starters, build a 100-square-foot, 50-degree (past vertical) overhanging wall. If space and money are available, add a slightly overhanging traverse wall and some roof climbing. Do this and you'll only need a commercial gym for occasional redpoint practice.

Before we move on to the details of the advanced program, I must emphasize the context. High-dose strength training is appropriate only for experienced climbers who possess highly developed technical skills. Indoor-wall training can elicit a great muscular response but it does little for training technique. Don't be surprised after an extended stretch of indoor training if your return outdoors feels a bit "off" at first. Rest assured your technical skills will dial in quickly (assuming you once owned them) and you'll be climbing better than ever, thanks to your new-found strength.

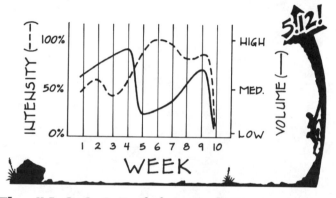

Intensity and volume of climbing and training during the ten-week "4-3-2-1 Cycle."

The "4-3-2-1 Training Cycle"

The practice of cyclic strength training has been around for decades. Applied to climbing there are several approaches. An excellent 18-week cycle is detailed in Tony Yaniro's and Steve Petro's *Fingers of Steel*. In this book I describe a 10-week cycle I developed, called the 4-3-2-1 cycle. This shorter cycle is mentally easier and may be more effective since you can train maximally on each workout day. (Longer training cycles require alternation of "easy" and "hard" days to prevent overtraining.)

Any training cycle of reasonable length will be somewhat effective as long as it possesses these four phases: endurance, maximum strength and power, anaerobic endurance, and rest. In the 10-week cycle, the length of each phase is four weeks, three weeks, two weeks, and one week, respectively. Each is detailed below.

Phase 1—Four Weeks of Forearm Endurance Training

The 4-3-2-1 cycle begins with the endurance "base" phase (weeks one through four). The focus here is on climbing—lots of it! During the "on" season, schedule regular weekend trips and log some redpoints. The off season may be spent mostly in your local climbing gym or on your home wall. Overall volume of climbing should crescendo toward week four, but workout intensity must remain in the mid-range at 40 to 70 percent. An occasional maximum intensity day (as in working a redpoint) won't hurt once a week as part of the high-volume scheme.

The endurance phase is the ideal time to work on new technical skills. Do this early in your training sessions or break your climbing day into two parts—a morning skill training workout and afternoon endurance session. Avoid steep, power-oriented routes as well as anything at your limit. You must not get sucked into high-volume, high-intensity training (phase 3) during these weeks. That'll break the cycle and lower or negate its effectiveness.

Instead overdose on long routes or traverses that are a couple grades below your limit. Aim for 60 to 90 minutes of nearly continuous climbing with the goal of *avoiding* a muscle-failing pump! This could be three 20- to 30-minute sets on your home wall with a 10-minute break, or twelve 6-minute gym routes with a just a minute or two of transition time between climbs. Whatever your approach, incorporate a 3 to 1 ratio of climbing to rest time.

Phase 2—Three Weeks of Finger Strength Training

Maximum finger strength is the most valuable commodity for high-end climbers. Assuming your head and technique are together, sending hard routes often comes down to your ability to stick small edges, pull shallow pockets, or hang onto slopers. As Yaniro points out, "If you cannot pull a single hard move, you have nothing to endure." Thus, strength training rules over endurance as declared in Absolute #6.

There has been much debate about the best method to train maximum finger strength. Bouldering has always been held high as a developer of finger strength. Fingerboards became popular in the late 1980s and are now joined by campus training in the 1990s. Although each of these methods are somewhat effective given the right program, they all fall short of being *the best* at developing maximum finger strength.

Efficacy of a finger strengthening exercise is dependent on four fundamental requisites. The more of these requisites met, the more dramatic the results. Here's a quick look at each:

During the four week first phase of the training cycle, log a lot of time at the crags. Climb for "mileage" and tick some redpoints. Here Jody Rozin is redpointing "The Pod" (5.13b) at Summerville Lake, West Virginia.

Photo: Eddie Whittemore collection

Finger Training Methods–How Do They Stack Up?

	#1-High Intensity?	#2-Rapid Failure?	#3-Specific Movement?	#4-Isolate Grips?
Bouldering	yes	maybe	yes	no
Fingerboard	yes	yes	no	yes
Campus training	yes	yes	no	maybe
Hypergravity Isolation Training (HIT)	yes	yes	yes	yes

1. The exercise must be high intensity throughout the entire set. Intensity directly relates to the number of muscular motor units recruited and neurological activity. An exercise performed at near 100 percent intensity throughout the set is the goal.

In climbing, higher intensity is created by increasing wall angle, decreasing hold size, and increasing speed of movement. As you get stronger, however, there's a definite limit to how far you can go with each of these variables—wall angles much past 45 degrees are too roof-like, very small holds are painful to train on, and climbing too fast fosters poor technique. When taken to extremes, all these adjustments will have a negative impact on your training.

A better method to up intensity is adding weight to your body. Any bodybuilder will tell you higher resistance equals higher intensity. Adding just 10 to 15 pounds causes a huge increase in intensity on overhanging walls and will yield a leap in finger strength in just a couple weeks. Interestingly, very few climbers are aware of this fact.

2. The exercise must produce muscular failure in less than one minute. It's universally accepted that strength training must produce muscular failure during the anaerobic phase of exercise. In the weight-lifting world, muscular failure in 6 to 12 reps is considered ideal. This is also valid for our sport but translates to high-intensity climbing that produces failure in 12 to 24 total hand movements. In climbing, however, there's always the lingering question of whether failure resulted from maxxed-out muscles or not being able to do a move.

3. The exercise must be specific to climbing positions and movements. Strength gains resulting from a certain exercise are specific to situations involving similar position and movement. The greater the difference between the exercise and sport use, the less the strength will transfer. Thus, the best strength training exercise for climbing would involve actual climbing movements, whereas an exercise performed while standing or hanging would transfer less.

4. The exercise must focus on a specific grip position for an entire set. In climbing, the rock dictates a random use of many different grip positions. Since strength is specific to each grip position, such cycling of grips allows you to climb much longer than if you use the same grip repeatedly. That's great if you are climbing for performance; but for the purpose of training grip strength it stinks! That's why a full season of climbing will build endurance, but leave you with the same maximum finger strength as the previous year.

Effective finger-strength training must hammer a specific grip until failure. Due to the limited transfer of strength from one grip to another, you'll need to train all the basic grip positions in this same manner. The six I suggest are open hand, crimp, pinch, and the three two-finger pocket "teams." Isolate and strengthen these grips, and there will be enough near transfer to cover just about any novel grip position you encounter on the rock.

Let's analyze three popular methods for strengthening the fingers plus a new exercise and protocol I've developed. How well each exercise method meets the fundamental requisites (discussed above) will determine its effectiveness.

A powerful boulder move at Fontainbleau, France.

BOULDERING: The common belief that bouldering is the *best* finger-strength exercise is wrong for two reasons. Failure may result from inability to do a move before you reach absolute muscular failure. Worse yet, bouldering inevitably involves a variety of grip positions. This "cycling" of grips is great for training endurance or anaerobic endurance but misses the mark for building maximum strength.

FINGERBOARD: Proper fingerboard training will develop some strength gains. A one-minute set of brief, repetitive, high-intensity hangs (add weight) on a single-grip position meets three of the four requirements. However, specificity to climbing movement is not satisfied due to the straight arms and dangling legs. This downfall limits transfer to the rock, but it's better than no finger training at all.

CAMPUS TRAINING: Campus training is the latest rage. Its high-intensity jumps and drops between holds maximally stimulate the neuromuscular system developing upper-body power and increasing contact strength—that's good. Like the fingerboard, however, it lacks specificity to body use on rock—that's not good. What's more, wooden-strip campus training focuses on the open-hand grip while neglecting others. For this reason, up-campusing on plastic holds (medium-sized and no sharp edges) is preferred since it offers a greater choice of grips to be trained. Meanwhile, drop-down campus training on wooden strips wins for pure recruitment and power. Thus, you'll get best results by mixing it up with both methods. Of course, campus training requires a significant base strength to get started. If you don't have a pretty savage grip already, it may feel impossible and is certainly dangerous.

Bob Africa powering one more Campus Training Repetition.

HYPERGRAVITY ISOLATION TRAINING (a.k.a. Hörst Isolation Training): Advanced climbers have experimented with weighted climbing for years—the results have been mixed and enthusiasm so-so. Hypergravity isolation training (HIT) is a refined, new, and exciting method of weighted climbing I developed over the last couple of years. HIT workouts meet all four of the above requisites and produce almost immediate quite noticeable gains in maximum finger strength! HIT involves high-intensity (adding weight simulates "hypergravity") climbing on *identical* HIT Strips™ mounted on a 50-degree overhanging wall. The early returns on its effectiveness have been enthusiastic thumbs up.

Even more exciting is that HIT workouts (unlike Campus Training) can be performed by all but beginner and severely out-of-shape climbers. Still, you must proceed carefully. This training method simulates hypergravity—greater than gravity's normal resistance to climbing—and thus is more stressful than normal climbing. HIT workouts are but *part* of a great overall training program and are best performed only during phase 2 of the 10-week training cycle. (See the Starter HIT Workouts on page 49.)

HYPERGRAVITY ISOLATION TRAINING (HIT)

Wall setup: Use an overhanging bouldering wall of three-quarter-inch plywood at an angle of 45 to 55 degrees past vertical. HIT workouts on a 55-degree (past vertical) wall are significantly harder than the common 45-degree wall. If you are building a wall for HIT workouts, I advise a compromised angle of 50 degrees—err on the side of too steep. Wall angles overhanging less than 45 degrees are not suggested for HIT workouts.

Sitting on the floor under the wall, mount the first HIT Strip™ at top-of-head height. Mount four more strips at 18-inch intervals. Two pinch holds are positioned above the first HIT Strip™ at shoulder width. The remaining pinch holds are mounted above the remaining HIT Strips™ at similar intervals.

HIT Principles and Tips:

1. Each set must be maximum intensity and produce failure in 24 hand movements or less. Add weight if you achieve more than 24 reps on any hold or set.
2. No stopping or chalking during a set. Climb briskly and without hesitation. If necessary get a spotter, but keep moving until the grip being trained fails.
3. Try to climb through the reps with normal foot movements and body turns. Smaller foot holds are better, but too much thought on footwork will slow you down. As long as it feels like climbing movements you are fine.
4. Rest breaks between sets must be exactly three minutes. Use a stopwatch and stick to the planned order and schedule of exercises. This way, at long last, you can quantify and track your finger strength! If you're sloppy on the length of rests, the numbers (weight added and reps) will lose meaning.
5. Keep a training book where you log each set, weight added, and reps performed. This way you'll always know what weight you need for a given set and you can easily track your gains (weight and rep increases) from workout to workout.
6. Always do your HIT workout in the same order and never increase the number of sets! There will be no added benefit, and you'll only dig yourself a deeper hole from which to recovery (that is, you'll need more days to recover).
7. Train with a partner for added energy and discipline. He or she can do their set during your three-minute rest interval and yell at you to "crank one more rep" during your set.
8. Consider taping your fingers. This is imperative when the weight added exceeds 20 pounds. Taping also increases skin comfort allowing you to push the envelope a bit farther with less pain.
9. HIT workouts are intense. Do no other serious climbing on HIT workout days. Always warm up and cool down properly. Consider soaking your hands in ice water for several minutes after the workout.

The Workout: Start with a 30-minute warmup consisting of stretching, self-massaging your fingers/forearms, and bouldering. Gradually, increase the intensity of the bouldering during the warm-up period. Take a 5- to 10-minute rest before beginning the HIT workout.

Six hand positions will be trained: crimp grip, pinch grip, the three "teams" of two-finger grips and the open-hand grip. Perform three sets for the crimp grip and two sets of the others. Start with the crimp grip.

Climber grabbing HIT Pinch Holds positioned between each HIT strip. Note: the HIT strips feature identical crimp, pocket and open-hand holds, fundamental to HIT workouts.

Sitting below the first HIT Strip™, place one hand (say right) on the right hand crimp edge on the strip. Start the stopwatch, then pull with your right hand and grab the left crimp edge of the second HIT Strip™. Continue climbing toward the fifth strip—right hand on third, left on fourth, right on fifth, then left hand on fifth. Begin descending immediately with the right grabbing fourth, left on third, right on second, left on first, then right on first. That's 11 total hand movements but keep going! Move your left hand up to the second strip, right to third, and continue on in the same fashion until the grip fails. Now that's how you fry a grip and increase its maximum strength!

If you do more than 24 reps, you must add weight. A little resistance makes a big difference. If you failed at just over 24 reps, add 2 or 4 pounds. If you sent 24 or more easily, then add 10 pounds for your next set. Although you can add weights to a climbing harness, I suggest a fanny pack and buy a dozen 2-pound diver's weights; you can also buy a diver's belt, although they're pricey. This makes adding or subtracting 2-pound weights quick and easy from set to set.

After your three-minute rest, proceed immediately with

a second crimp-grip set. Go until failure. Rest exactly three minutes, crank out the final crimp set and take another three-minute rest before moving on to the pinch-grip position.

Perform the two-pinch-grip sets in the exact manner described above. Always take a three-minute rest between sets.

The two-finger pocket "teams" are next. Do two sets of each beginning with the "third team". This is the weakest grip, which uses the pinky and ring finger. Don't be surprised if at first you can only do 10 or 12 hand movements at body weight. This grip will strengthen rapidly and you'll soon be adding weight.

The "second team" two-finger combo is the index and middle finger. Do two sets of these, then two sets with the strongman "first team" of middle fingers. Rests between all sets remain three minutes throughout.

Conclude you HIT workout by hammering the open-hand grip with two sets to failure. Do no further climbing except for 10 minutes of light cool-down bouldering and as always finish you workout with three sets of reverse wrist curls. All that's needed now are two to three days of quality rest and sound nutrition, and your grip will recover far stronger than ever before!

STARTER HIT WORKOUTS – Novice and Expert

grip to work	weight added* for HIT "novice"	weight added* HIT "expert"	reps** and rest interval
crimp (set 1)	10 lbs.	24 lbs.	<24 & 3 mins.
crimp (set 2)	10 lbs.	24 lbs.	<24 & 3 mins.
crimp (set 3)	10 lbs.	24 lbs.	<24 & 3 mins.
pinch (set 1)	none	10 lbs.	<24 & 3 mins.
pinch (set 2)	none	10 lbs.	<24 & 3 mins.
2-F "3rd team" (set 1)	none	10 lbs.	<24 & 3 mins.
2-F "3rd team" (set 2)	none	10 lbs.	<24 & 3 mins.
2-F "2nd team" (set 1)	6 lbs.	20 lbs.	<24 & 3 mins.
2-F "2nd team" (set 2)	6 lbs.	20 lbs.	<24 & 3 mins.
2-F "1st team" (set 1)	8 lbs.	24 lbs.	<24 & 3 mins.
2-F "1st team" (set 2)	8 lbs.	24 lbs.	<24 & 3 mins.
open hand (set 1)	14 lbs.	30 lbs.	<24 & 3 mins.
open hand (set 2)	14 lbs.	30 lbs.	<24 & 3 mins.

*   Lower weight or stop training at the first sign of tendon or joint pain.
** End every set at 24 reps or failure, whichever comes first. If you reach 24 reps, add weight for the next set and/or next workout. Keep a training log with the details of each HIT workout.

HIT Strips™ are available from NICROS (1-800-699-1975).

Phase 3—Two Weeks of Anaerobic-Endurance Training

Assuming you have enough strength to do the individual moves on a route, it's your anaerobic endurance (a.k.a. power endurance or power stamina) that's put to the test. Nontop (no shakes) difficult bouldering with muscular failure in approximately five minutes is the preferred method. Vary the intensity of the movements back and forth between 60 and 95 percent. This is much like interval training used by runners and is excellent for developing anaerobic endurance. Your goal is to prolong a maximal burn as long as possible.

Interestingly, many climbers already train this way on indoor bouldering caves and at their home crags. Why then don't they all become super strong and end up sending 5.12s in their sleep?

Answer: Anaerobic endurance training places high levels of stress on the nervous system and muscles. Beyond a certain point the body cannot recover from these workouts. About two weeks seems to be the limit if you climb regularly. Ironically, many climbers train this way for months on end and then wonder why they don't get stronger. Undoubtedly, they are overtraining, and injury, sickness, and depression may be the legacy of such training.

Todd Skinner spots Scott Milton on one of the countless powerful bouldering routes at Hueco Tanks, Texas.

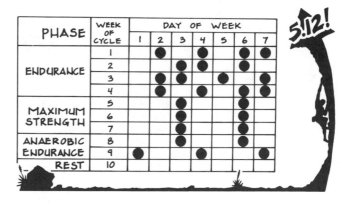

PHASE	WEEK OF CYCLE	1	2	3	4	5	6	7
ENDURANCE	1		●		●		●	●
	2			●	●			
	3			●	●	●		●
	4			●		●		● ●
MAXIMUM STRENGTH	5			●			●	
	6			●			●	
	7			●				
ANAEROBIC ENDURANCE	8			●			●	
	9	●			●			●
REST	10							

Phase 4—One Week of Rest and Recovery

Much of the efficacy of the 10-week cycle depends on your discipline to finish it up with a full week off from training. During the nine preceding weeks, you hit your body relentlessly two to four days per week. Although one to three days rest between individual workouts is usually enough for muscular recovery, wear and tear on the joints and tendons, and mental fatigue continue to accumulate. This rest week goes a long way to clear the slate of mental fatigue, as well as give connective tissues time to "catch up" in the healing and recovery process.

At the end of your rest week, evaluate your mental and physical state. If you're not feeling 100 percent ready to go, take another 3 to 14 days off. An extra week or two invested in healing a finger-tendon strain has greater long-term value than the few workouts you'll miss. Any loss of strength or skill during this time off will also be negligible.

PREVENTING INJURY AND SPEEDING RECOVERY

Supplemental Training for Muscle Balance

Climbing works the finger-flexor muscles to death but does little to strengthen the extensor muscles on the back of your forearms or the pronators. These growing imbalances leave you susceptible to elbow tendinitis.

Reverse wrist curls are a great exercise that will help prevent lateral epicondylitis—inflammation of the tendon origin of the forearm extensors and more popularly known as tennis elbow. Perform these curls religiously at the end of each workout to strengthen your forearm extensors. Three, 25-rep sets with a light weight will do the trick. (See supplemental exercises on pages 38 to 40.)

For the pronators you can do a simple pronation exercise

Push-Muscle Exercises

1. Push-ups or light bench press. Three sets of standard push-ups, once or twice a week is enough. Vary the distance between hands if you like and always go until failure. If you prefer to use a bench press—fine. But keep the weights light and reps high. It's inadvisable to use much more than 75 percent of your body weight.

2. Light shoulder press. Use dumbbells, a light bar or a machine and perform three sets of around 20 reps. Total resistance should be limited to between 30 and 40 percent of your body weight. Do these, once to, at most, twice per week.

3. Dips. Somewhat similar to mantles when performed with your hand in close to your body. Three sets to failure, once or twice per week is ideal. Have a spotter aid you if initially you can't do at least 10 reps.

with a lightly weighted 12-inch section of broomstick. (See the photograph on page 40.) These are best performed as a warm-up exercise before climbing to help prevent medial epicondylitis.

Maintaining some semblance of balance in the larger muscles of your upper body is also important. The pull muscles become monstrously strong from climbing, while the push muscles such as the pectorals, deltoids, and triceps fall behind. Push-ups and dips are two exercises that will compensate in these areas without adding much mass. Two sets each, once or twice a week is usually enough. This "minimalist" approach for push-muscle training is ideal, so there's no need for any free-weight training.

Rest and Recovery from Workouts

As Absolute #8 pointed out, training does not produce muscular growth or gains in strength. It merely stimulates the body's growth mechanisms into motion. In fact, high-intensity training like the maximum strength and anaerobic endurance phases of the 4-3-2-1 cycle are severely catabolic (muscle eating) and fry the nervous system. It's during rest that your body recovers and with enough rest rebuilds to a higher level than before.

It's very common for enthusiastic climbers to workout again before completion of the recovery process. Although you may get away with this once or twice (and with little benefit from your workouts), you will quickly fall into the downward spiral of overtraining. In my opinion, a good definition of insanity is the continuation of training that produces no obvious, or even negative, results.

Quality rest is key to getting stronger, but the exact amount is hard to pin down. There are many factors that contribute to rate of recovery such as your diet, hours of sleep, rest-day activity, and level of fitness. Another major factor is the intensity-level of the workout. Complete recovery from a low-intensity endurance workout may take just 24 hours while a savage two-hour anaerobic endurance workout could take up to five days. Ultimately, you need to be aware of your body's signals and continue with your next workout only when you're back to 100 percent.

Nutrition to Speed Recovery

Your muscles cannot begin rebuilding until you go to sleep, but they can begin restocking glycogen (sugar fuel in the muscle). You can shorten recovery time by starting the glycogen repletion process during cool down. Sports drinks containing a mixture of glucose, sucrose, and glucose polymers absorb most rapidly. Low-fat candy is the next best source of simple sugar. Consume between 50 and 150 grams depending on the length and intensity of your workout. And don't delay; to get this head start on recovery, you must ingest the sugar upon completion of the workout.

Next, you need high-quality protein and complex carbohydrates within two hours after your workout. Drink 30 grams of liquid protein (ion-exchange whey or egg albumen) to provide the building blocks. Whole-food protein is less desirable since it's slower to digest. A moderate serving of vegetables and pasta will meet your carbohydrate requirements providing an extended "trickle" of sugar into the body for several

Injury Prevention and Recovery Tips

• Train your antagonistic muscles frequently to help ward off injury. Consider mandatory three sets of pronators before each workout and three sets of reverse wrist curls at the end of every training session. A few sets of push-ups and dips each week are also advised.

• Quality rest is as important as quality stimulus (the workout) for producing gains in strength. Don't proceed with your next workout until fully recovered. Use muscle soreness and your overall energy level to gauge where you are in the recovery process. A written record tracking workouts, sleep, diet, and how you "feel" will improve awareness on this matter.

• Your dietary habits following a workout are key to minimizing recovery time and maximizing muscular restructuring. Consume 100 grams of simple carbohydrates upon completion of your workout. Follow this with 30 grams of liquid protein and a moderately sized carbohydrate meal within two hours.

• At least nine hours of sleep is required for optimal recovery from severe workouts. About eight hours is optimal on other nights.

High-intensity climbing can easily lead to overtraining or injury without adequate rest and nutrition. A most stressful day of climbing or training should be followed by a minimum of two days rest.

Photo: Mike McGill

hours. Eat additional small "meals" of carbohydrates every few hours to keep the "trickle" going. This is especially important in the 24 hours following a hard workout.

Sleep and Grow Strong

The body repairs itself and new growth takes place only as you sleep. Therefore, the amount of sleep the night of a hard workout is as important as your use of proper training exercises and consumption of correct nutrients. Studies of thousands of athletes in many different sports show a dramatic difference in the rate of recovery in those getting nine hours sleep as opposed to only six. What's more, athletes sleeping nine hours were less likely to get injured or suffer from overtraining.

Granted, if your schedule is anything like mine there are too few hours in the day already. The good news is the largest sleep requirement is the first night after intense exercise. If at all possible get eight and a half to nine hours that night. Go to bed earlier as opposed to sleeping in later to log the extra time. Try for seven and a half to eight hours sleep on the second night, and between six and eight on all successive nights until your next workout. Remember, sleep is an essential part of your training. Don't hesitate to say "no" to late night outings and other Bohemian activities in favor of getting stronger, faster!

Finally, if you workout in the morning or do split workouts, consider a 30- to 60-minute nap during the day. This too may be hard to pull off, but along with the nutritional regime discussed above, provides the greatest training and recovery effects.

Mike Freeman on
"Nector Vector" (5.12),
Shawawangunks, New
York.

Photo: Michael Miller

Winning the Head Games

*I wanna do something absolutely at my limit,
where my whole body is screaming in pain,
everything wants to fall off, but I keep on
going.*

—Jerry Moffatt

It's the head games that separate the men (and women) from the boys in this sport. Physical and technical prowess can collapse without a moment's notice if you don't possess a "good head." A well-known climbing axiom is that "the greatest ascents result more often from mental breakthroughs than physical." Consider the focus and vision of Wolfgang Gullich sending the steep, one-finger pocketed Action Direct (5.14d) back in 1991; the unwavering motivation and discipline of Lynn Hill to free climb the 3,000-foot Nose of El Capitan in a day; and the laser-like concentration and confidence of John Gill's 1961 solo of the Thimble (5.11d) while wearing hiking boots nonetheless. Such legendary accomplishments are the result of the synergy of skill, fitness, and mental fortitude. Greatness comes no other way.

In this chapter, I touch on 11 elements of the head game. Clearly all are intertwined, but I've broken them down into more bite-sized chucks and present them in a logical progression. As you read, reflect on your personal head games and consider what improvements can be made. Employ the "tip" after each section to begin the journey toward some legendary accomplishments of your own!

MOTIVATION MULTIPLIES TALENT

Motivation is the foundation for all accomplishments. Natural talent, great genetics, and all the time and money in the world will get you nowhere without motivation. Many great human feats are achieved by modestly talented, even disabled, persons who possess heroic levels of motivation. Consider Oprah Winfrey running a full marathon, or more seriously, Hugh Herr climbing a 5.13 just two years after the amputation of his lower legs. Now that takes motivation!

Consistent, day-to-day motivation to train hard and to push yourself at the crags is a common problem. External stimuli like aggro tunes or a double espresso merely energize your state at that moment—they do not motivate. Motivation is a 24-hour focus and enthusiasm to do the things that help you toward your goal, while steering clear of anything that might

Climbing "Stage Fright" (5.12d X) took extreme motivation for Hugh Herr, who lost his lower legs in a mountaineering accident in 1982.

Photo: Peter Lewis

slow the process. Ultimately, it's your expectations and incentives that keep the motivation burning.

Always expect success whether you're training or climbing. In the gym, expect that the workout will make you stronger and elevate you toward your goals. At the crags, expect you'll send the route—or at least learn a new skill that will make a difference in the future. Believe there's a positive causal connection between the task at hand and your future goals, and motivation will be yours. Oppositely, even a fleeting thought that the workout won't help or success is not likely will hose motivation in an instant.

Incentives to train also enhance motivation. Simple things such as a tick list of to-do routes, a competition you've entered, or a road trip inked in on the calendar will stoke the fires. As the tick-list routes begin to fall or as the competition nears, your motivation will grow stronger still.

Finally, there's the power of visualization to motivate. Whether the task is six months of writing a book about climbing 5.12 or six months training to climb a 5.12, daily visualization of the completed project will power consistent action.

Tip: Unwavering motivation is fundamental to realizing athletic potential. To this end, create incentives to train, expect success as you climb, and begin with the end in mind and motivation will always be yours.

GOALS THAT COMPEL ACTION

Most people set goals in the long term—a dream climb, place, event, maybe even grade level of climbing. But to set only long-term goals is to miss the boat to them altogether. In fact, short-term goals are more powerful as they fuel and steer your boat toward long-term destinations. Start your trek today by establishing some written goals in three time frames: short term (daily), medium term (weekly or monthly), and long term.

Short-term goals are simply a daily to-do list specific to improving your climbing performance. Write them down the night before or as you eat breakfast in the morning. Here are a few examples: If yesterday was a savage maximum-strength workout, your list reads "eat five small carbohydrate and protein meals and get eight and a half hours of sleep." Or if you have a climbing gym workout scheduled today, set goals specific to training weaknesses, new skills, and a few strength exercises. At the crags, write down the warm-up exercises and routes to do before attempting your redpoint project. No matter what the task, a written list, whether on a Post-it™ note or in a training log, is the carrot compelling consistent, intelligent actions.

Medium-term planning integrates your training and climbing schedule with the rest of your life. It will optimize your use of time and keep you on the fast track to higher performance. Loosely plan things out on a calendar a few months in advance. First mark in big events such as climbing trips, competitions, work and family obligations, and so forth. Now plot the weekly phases of your training cycle, hopefully fitting them around your big events. In pencil, mark proposed workout, climbing, and rest days realizing that these days are flexible and can be changed. Finish by jotting down some specific physical and technical gains, as well as a couple routes you'd like to send in the coming months. Things such as "20 consecutive pull-ups," "improve finger-jamming technique," and "climb the Naked Edge" give additional meaning to the daily grind of training.

When all the important items are in place, the many little, less-important things in life can fall in where time allows. I'm talking about the myriad of distractions vying for your attention and time—television, parties, surfing the Net, and so forth. Although many persons can be "drugged" by the instant gratification they offer, medium-term planning will help keep you on track toward more lofty, meaningful accomplishments.

Finally, there are the long-term "dream" goals floating around in your mind. This might be the "grade" of climbing to achieve or a specific dream climb. Also, think about where you'd go if time and money weren't an issue. Is there an exotic climbing area you want to travel to? For any chance they will ever become reality, you must liberate them from the "dreamland" of your mind and put them down in black and white. There's a magical power in writing things down: It makes them believable and therefore achievable.

Tip: Detailed goals compel consistent daily and long-term action. Ask yourself, "What can I do in the next hour, day, week, month, or year to enhance my climbing performance?" Set short-, medium-, and long-term goals accordingly.

DISCIPLINE LEADS TO EXCELLENCE

To excel in anything—sport, business, relationships—takes a lot of discipline. Discipline to do all things that point toward your goal and discipline to abstain from the things that will move you away from it. When it comes to discipline there's no hi-tech, scientific gobbledygook to talk about; it just comes down to how badly you want it. There are many talented climbers who never became great because they lack discipline—for every two steps forward they take at least one step back. Conversely, many climbers of average talent have become masters of rock because they cut ties to anything that might hold them back. In the long run their sacrifices paid off by realizing their full potential in this sport.

Certainly discipline alone does not guarantee success; however, a lack of discipline goes a long way to guarantee you will fall short of your potential. Examine your discipline by asking yourself these questions.

1. Do I set daily goals that I usually meet?
2. Do I work out and climb only when my body is "ready," and take another rest day when I'm still fatigued or sore?
3. Do I most often say "no" to food and drink that can separate me from my goals, while supplying my body with the fuel and nutrients necessary to train hard and recover quickly?
4. Do I regularly sacrifice the late night social outings of the crowd for the good night's sleep of a serious athlete?
5. Do I hang out and climb with positive, motivated people who will help me toward my goals and avoid those with attitudes and habits that will hold me back?

Tip: Discipline is fundamental in the pursuit of excellence. Always distinguish between what's important and what's urgent—they are not the same! Favor activities and practices that carry you toward your goal, and only occasionally partake in gluttony as a well-deserved reward upon reaching a medium-term goal.

CRANKING UP CONFIDENCE

As much as any other attribute, your level of confidence upon starting a route may predetermine your likelihood of success. Think back to the last time you did a route you had wired. As you prepared for the climb, chances are you felt "no doubt" about the results and that "the route was in the bag." You then, of course, proceeded to send the route in a relaxed, carefree, yet focused state. This experience reflects the dramatic effect confidence has on performance. But what exactly is confidence and how is it developed?

Confidence is positive energy, enthusiasm and high expectancy of success. You climb free, loose, quick, and fluid, and even in the face of pressure, remain mentally calm and focused. However, such bullet-proof confidence does not just appear on the spot by thinking positive thoughts or hoping for the best. Confidence is developed beforehand via extensive preparation and experience.

Nothing elicits confidence like having been there before. Thus, one of your training goals should be to mimic as best as you can the atmosphere, situations, and terrain of the project or competition for which you're preparing. One great example of this is my friend Mike Freeman's training regimen for the steep, cavernous "Hole" at the New River Gorge. Noting his discomfort and intimidation the first time he attempted a route out the 30-foot roof, he set out to hang upside down under any object he could find in his hometown in New Jersey. With only

*Beth Rodden at
Nationals in 1996.*

*Confidence is key
whether at the crags or
in a competition.*

Photo: Stewart Green

marginal indoor walls in his area, he logged some time a few
days a week, climbing the underside on a playground jungle
gym. Although the physical training value of this was minimal,
the time spent in the horizontal developed familiarity with the
position and thus tremendous confidence. Confidence is a self-
fulfilling prophecy, and Mike went on to redpoint a number of
hard routes in the "hole" that season.

Physical and mental training also build confidence. The
strong, dialed-in feeling upon completing a 10-week training
cycle makes you more confident on the rock. You can also
bolster confidence on the spot by visualizing yourself sending
the route or by envisioning past successful climbs of similar
type and difficulty. If you feel there's a chink in your armor,
adjust or beef up your training program accordingly, as it will
serve to crank up your confidence.

**Tip: Confidence is essential to peak performance.
Always acclimate yourself to the conditions under
which you will perform. Use mock events, trial runs,
and simulator routes to help build confidence.**

VISUALIZATION—
PREPROGRAMMING THE FUTURE

Visualization is a fundamental skill used by top athletes the world over. If you're not actively using visualization, you're missing out on the most powerful smart bomb in a climber's arsenal.

Although similar to the mental rehearsals performed by many climbers, visualization goes beyond the simple task of reviewing sequences. With it you create detailed movies in your head with touch, sound, color and all the kinesthetic "feel" of doing a route. These movies aren't just colorful daydreams; they actually help build a mental map to a future, desired reality. Once programmed into the brain, these movies improve your mind/body integration, thereby enhancing your performance on the rock. Your movies become blueprints for action, so make sure they're positive and very detailed. Run and rerun the movies in your mind's eye, and soon they'll become a physical reality!

Visualization can enhance your climbing no matter the situation, whether in competition, on-sight or working a redpoint. The latter situation is the best for developing the skill. Having already "worked" a route, you should be able to vividly imagine the feeling of doing the moves, grabbing the holds, milking rests, and so forth. Remember, simply reviewing a sequence in your mind is not visualization. Make a movie complete with sound, color and touch. The more detailed the visualization, the more hard wired the moves will become.

You can also use visualization on routes you've never been on before. The world's best on-sight climbers have mastered the skill of creating a detailed movie of a successful attempt. Some persons even create two possible movies of crux sections and then select the one that looks most promising at the time. Study the climb from a few different ground perspectives noting possible rests, gear placements and, of course, looking for hidden holds and crux sequences. From these data begin to "shoot" a movie, first watching yourself climb the route, then feeling and experiencing yourself doing it in the movie.

The above strategy is invaluable for competition climbing. During your "preview" of the route, gather as much information and "shoot" as many pictures as possible. In isolation, build your mental movie and run through it in preparation for a flash ascent!

Another popular use of visualization is to "climb" during rest days. Or if you're laid up due to injury, regular visualization of a familiar route or your project helps maintain motor skills and route knowledge. A final at-the-crag use is to mentally send your project a few more times when you're physically too burned to climb any more. The above uses of visualization are certainly more beneficial than doing nothing at all.

Use of the many applications of visualization will dramatically improve your performance in both the short and long

Visualization Tips

1. Practice visualization with all your senses. Work on developing your ability to create crisp, clear mental pictures of people, places, and events.

2. Imagine scenes in explicit detail. The more vivid the images, the more powerful the effects visualization will have on your performance.

3. Use photographs, beta sheets, or videotape to improve the accuracy of the mental movies of your climbing.

4. Repeatedly visualize the project or sequences you're having trouble with. Mental practice of a sequence combined with physical practice of the same will yield better results than physical practice alone.

5. Create and store positive images for recall in countering negative pictures, thoughts, or feelings.

6. Create mental movies of yourself dealing with various situations or problems that might arise while on a climb.

7. Work every day to reconstruct negative and self-defeating images of yourself into positive and constructive ones.

8. Most importantly, establish a visualization practice schedule just as you plan out a regular gym-training schedule. For best results, practice your visualization while in a relaxed state and a quiet place (use the relaxation sequence detailed on page 68). Five or six short sessions of 5 or 10 minutes are better that just one or two long sessions per week.

term. Always dovetail visualization with actual climbing and training to maintain accuracy of the images and work to become acutely aware of the "feelings" and results you get. The more you practice visualization the sooner you'll master this vital skill.

Tip: Visualization helps preprogram future realities. Use it daily in preparation for training, climbing or any other important task. Draw all your senses into the images and allow yourself to feel the moves in motion. Make the images as positive and accurate as possible, as visualization can program both good and bad outcomes.

DEVELOPING PRECLIMB RITUALS

Rituals are powerful anchors for consistent performance. Rituals are used by all elite athletes. Observe Andre Agassi before every serve, the Shark before every tee shot, or Michael Jordan before every foul shot—their preparation and setup is identical each time. Every tiny detail is programmed into a mental "checklist" including posture, breathing, visualization and final thoughts. For these athletes, habitual rituals produce consistently positive results.

Develop your own rituals based on past experiences. Whether a list of activities or meals and a "to bed" time for the day before a competition or a tick list of preclimb preparations, consistent rituals yield consistent results. What did you do and think in the minutes leading up to some of your particularly brilliant ascents? What did you do the day before the climb that helped maximize your energy and mental state? Awareness of all the little things is key! The more detailed and lengthy the rituals the greater the affect. Include everything you can think of from when and how you lace your shoes, to tying into the rope, to chalking up and taking a few slow, deep breaths before you start climbing. You may even want to model some elements of rituals performed by other successful climbers.

Precompetition rituals are especially useful as time markers leading up to a competition. The ritual may begin days before the event and count down to the minutes before the climb as you perform your warmup, stretching, visualization, and preparatory self-talk. As you step up to the wall your focus will be laser-like and your confidence high, knowing your tried and true ritual has placed you in the ideal performance state of past successes.

Tip: Consistent preclimb rituals give birth to consistent performances. Establish a detailed preclimb routine including all preparatory tasks from gearing up to mental rehearsal. When the ritual becomes tried and true, stick to it! If you are a competition climber, develop a separate precompetition ritual beginning several days before the competition and continuing down to the moment you get on the wall.

REASONABLE FEARS VERSUS UNREASONABLE FEARS

The no-fear mentality is for buffoons, beer-guzzling frat boys, and couch potatoes. In climbing, reasonable fears keep you alive long enough to realize your potential and to send a long lifetime's worth of stellar routes. For example, fear of taking a ground fall compels you to seek good protection on the lead and to drag a rope in the first place.

It's *unreasonable* fears that derail performance. Things such as fear of falling on a well-protected route, fear of performance pains, fear of failure, and fear of embarrassment

"Hang on BP!," in Berks County, Pennsylvania.
Photo: Mike McGill

must all be nixed. There are also preclimb fears such as "I might be too tall," "too short," or "too weak" to do the climb—left unchecked, these fears give birth to reality. Finally, there are subconscious, preprogrammed fears that are the root of many of the "dumb things" that seem to just "happen." Have you ever fallen after the crux when the route is in the bag? Or have you slipped off a large hold or botched a wired sequence even though you felt in control? It may be that such mistakes are the result of unchallenged inner fears, not lack of ability.

Deal with your fears head on. Start by writing down recurrent fears that regularly hurt your performance. If you can't think of any on the spot, go for a climb and pay special attention to every preclimb thought and while-you-climb concern. As the fears reveal themselves, use logic and reason to specifically counter each. This is usually pretty easy, but if no logical counter is evident, the fear may be *reasonable*.

Dealing with fear is an ongoing process—our fears are always changing. Review each poor performance and identify which fear(s) may have contributed to your difficulties. To help you with this analysis, here's a primer on four basic climbing fears: fear of falling, fear of pain, fear of failure, and fear of embarrassment.

Fear of Falling. Fear of falling is inherent to climbing. Interestingly enough, it's not really falling that we fear but not knowing what the fall will be like. This explains why your first fall on a route is the scariest, while subsequent falls are often much less stressful. Beginners probably need some hands-on proof that falls can be safe. The best way for a would-be leader to gain trust in the system is by taking some intentional falls. Find a steep climb with good protection, use a good rope (and double check your knot and buckle) and take some falls. Start off with 2-footers and build up to 15-footers. A more experienced climber fearful of falling on an upcoming on-sight climb can counter the fear during the preclimb warmup. The tactic here is to mentally replay some past inconsequential falls and remind yourself that falls on this climb will be no different (if that is indeed the case—some falls are obviously deadly and only a fool would ignore that possibility).

Fear of Pain. When pushing your limits, fear of pain and discomfort can become a critical weakness. This fear causes you to give up long before your body has reached its physical limitations. The pain of climbing a continuously strenuous route is akin to that of running a mile at full speed—it freaking hurts! Fortunately, the pain is brief and the challenge pays big dividends. Decide to push yourself a bit farther into the discomfort zone each time you're on a hard route. Soon your pain threshold will be redefined, as will your limits on the rock!

Fear of Failure. This deep-seated fear is instilled during childhood when almost every action is classified by our family, teachers and friends as either a success or a failure. We've all had childhood situations where the fear of failure was so gripping we became immobilized and time seemed to stop. Fortunately, adults generally don't react quite that intensely, but it is still common for us to imagine all the bad things that could possibly go wrong. Once triggered, these negative thoughts can snowball and, more often than not, become self-fulfilling prophecies.

In climbing, fear of failure causes you to hold back. Your attack on a route becomes less aggressive than required, you'll find yourself second-guessing sequences in the midst of doing them and your breathing will become shallow and your grip will tighten. You may even fall prey to "paralysis by analysis."

Eliminate fear of failure one of two ways. First, focus on what is probable instead of what is possible. Sure, it's human nature to always consider the worst case scenario, but it almost never comes true. Counter these thoughts by considering what is probable and realistic based on past experiences. The second method to nix this fear is to focus all your attention on the process of climbing and forget about the possible outcomes. Concentrate on the things immediate to your performance like precise foot placements, relaxing your grip, moving quickly onto the next rest position, and so forth. Your limited supply of energy is too valuable to waste worrying about how high you will climb or the eventual results. Let that take care of itself.

Remember that in sports there are no failures, only results. If you fall off the first move of a route, it is a result of not paying attention to the move, not because you are a worthless individual. The results might not be ideal, but they do contain hints for improvement. It is through your failures that you grow as a climber and a person.

Fear of Embarrassment. Finally, there is fear of embarrassment. Get over this now, or you'll never fully enjoy this sport nor reach your potential. Occasional bad performance days are inevitable. Instead of trying to avoid them, simply accept that they happen, analyze why they happened, then bury them. With this attitude you will be free to try chancy moves and risk an occasional mistake. In the long run you'll often look like a hero and only occasionally like a zero. Surely this is better than embracing the critics and accepting mediocrity all the time.

Don't forget your friends know how good a climber you are, and they won't think any worse of you because of a poor performance. Anyone else critical of you really doesn't matter. Work on improving your self-confidence and don't let the criticisms of others invade your thoughts. As the Flash Training bumper sticker says, "JUST SEND IT!"

Tip: Determine whether your fears are reasonable or unreasonable. Heed the reasonable fears, but challenge and laugh in the face of your unreasonable fears. Relaxation and reason are an effective antidote to most unfounded fears encountered on the rock. Focus on what is probable not on the worst case scenario, which is only slightly possible.

TURNING DOWN THE PRESSURE

Pressure is not inherently good or bad. It's your ability to control and react to pressure that determines its value. You've probably experienced high-pressure situations where nervousness, anxiety, tightness, and lack of focus prevailed, ultimately dooming your performance. Times like these make you dream of "no pressure" situations—surely that would be the ideal. Right?

Well, actually not. Some degree of pressure is good. It energizes you and enhances your focus on the task at hand. Remember, the pressure of cramming the night before a big exam? Moderate pressure acts as a bit of a "stick," and when combined with a tasty "carrot" (the goal) the results can be stellar. Learning to use this "good" pressure and to eliminate "bad" pressure is key.

The control knob to pressure is completely in your hands! Realize that while you will never have control over all ele-

Relaxation Sequence

Perform the following procedure at least once a day, ideally in a quiet, dimly lit room. Allow 15 minutes at first, but with practice you'll be able to reach a state of complete relaxation in less than 5 minutes. This sequence requires you to tense, then relax various muscles in your body. Note the difference in feeling in a tense versus a completely relaxed muscle. Awareness is everything!

Go through the sequence in this exact order trying to flex only the muscle(s) specified in each step (a valuable skill you will master quickly). Perform the sequence lying or sitting in a comfortable position. Spend about one minute on each step.

1. With eyes closed, take five deep breaths. Inhale slowly over five seconds, then exhale to a silent 10 count.

2. Tense the muscles in your lower legs (one leg at a time) for five seconds. Let go of the contraction and feel the tension release. Focus on total relaxation of the muscles; feel them become "light and airy."

3. Now do the same sequence with the muscles of the upper leg. Tense only those muscles and hold for five seconds. Relax and feel the tension drain away. Remain focused on the relaxed feeling of the muscles. Do not let your thoughts stray. After a minute move on to the next body part.

4. The arms are next, starting below the elbow. Make a tight fist for five seconds and release. Allow your fingers and hands to fall completely relaxed.

5. Now tense the muscles of the upper arm, one at a time. Try to tense/relax the biceps and triceps separately. Spend at least one minute on this step.

6. Now tense the muscles of the torso for five seconds, then relax. As you get better, try to tense the chest, shoulder, back, and abdominal muscles separately.

7. Finish by tensing the muscles of the face and neck. Relax them completely, remaining aware of true feeling of relaxation.

8. Concentrate on relaxing all the muscles in your body. Mentally scan from head to toe for any muscles that might still contain tension. Maintain this state of total relaxation for at least three minutes.

9. Open your eyes, stretch, and feel refreshed, or begin visualization training. If you're tired, crash a while.

ments of a situation, you do have control over your reactions to them. Psychologists explain that no one makes you feel pressure, fear, anger, or frustration but you. Either you allow yourself to feel that way, or you empower someone else to make you feel that way. Acknowledge that you are at the helm of your emotions. Work for constant awareness of how you feel and why. Only then can you make the necessary changes to foster optimal performance.

Let's consider a few ways to optimize pressure in stressful climbing situations, whether at the crag preparing for a redpoint or in isolation at a competition. The goal is to maintain positive pressures while eliminating negative pressures.

Positive pressure evolves from effective preparations leading up to the event. For instance, a good training program, sound nutrition, proper rest, and a good support team will leave you anticipating a solid, successful performance. You'll be focused and optimistic, ready to get to the climb and shred. Such positive pressure is the antithesis of the dread, anxiety, and negative attitude that can result from poor preparations like training too little (or more likely overtraining), too little sleep, and poor nutrition.

Assuming you make it to the event positive and upbeat, your next goal is to maintain this state and ward off all the negative pressures trying to infect you. A solid and very detailed preclimb ritual goes a long way toward this end. However, some negative tension or anxiety is often impossible to avoid. Use relaxation (see relaxation sequence on opposite page) to deflate such negative pressure and maintain your ideal performance state.

Tip: Moderate pressure—not the absence of pressure—produces top performances. Learn to foster good pressure and nix bad pressure as you are in the driver's seat. Your actions and thoughts in the days and hours leading up to the event determine your pressure levels. Use relaxation as your on-the-spot antidote to negative pressures that try to invade.

FOCUS—THE MIND'S HOLD ON THE ROCK

The ability to narrow and maintain focus is an invaluable mental skill. Widely used, but often misunderstood in the context of a climber's lexicon, the word "focus" means a laser-like concentration of mental energy placed on the most important task at any given instant. Since, in climbing, every movement possesses a different most-important task, you must learn to direct and redirect pinpoint focus on the specific finger or foot placement most critical at each instant.

Think about focus as a narrowing of your concentration. Much like a zoom lens on a camera, you must zoom in and magnify a specific, critical task—toeing in on a small pocket, placing and pulling on a manky finger jam, or shifting your weight to just the right balance point. Without this tight focus your foot may pop or your hand may slip or overgrip and chance of failure increases.

The most difficult part of focus is learning to zoom in and out quickly from a pinpoint focus to a more wide-angle perspective. The wide-angle mode is used when scooping a sequence ahead and planning a strategy. When climbing,

Practice focus training in the safe, controlled environment of a gym, and in time it will be yours on crag projects and in competitions.

Forty-something Steve Hong focuses and flashes another competition route!

Photo: Stewart Green

zoom in tightly as you high-step on a dime edge, lock-off a hold, or float a deadpoint. The key is learning to switch your point of focus rapidly—much like a laser light show—from one critical task to the next. All the while you ward off outside distractions that threaten to grab and divert your focus away from the rock—certainly not the easiest job in the world. The good news is there's a prescription to improve your focus. No, not Ritalin, but a simple "focus-training" exercise you can use at the gym or crag.

Train focus on a route you know or one graded well below your top level. Climb the whole route (ideally on toprope) while trying to maintain focus on a single aspect of movement. For instance, focus only on hand placements. As you climb, find the best way to grab each hold, use the minimum amount of grip strength to stick it and feel how your purchase changes as you pull on the hold (for example, can you relax your grip more with changing body position or must it tighten?). Place as little focus as is safely possible in other areas like your feet, balance, belayer, and so forth. For now, these areas must take care of themselves; let your sixth sense handle the job.

This exercise is indeed difficult. Your thoughts will wander and distractions from the ground will occasionally grab your attention. When this occurs, simply redirect your focus to the predetermined task and continue on. Part of the benefit of this exercise is sharpened awareness of when focus is lost and the ability to return it to the desired task. Repeat this drill regularly but with different focus (feet, weight shifts, relaxed movement, and so forth) each time. Work to increase the length of time you can maintain a singular focus. This builds mental endurance. Eventually, you can modify the exercise by switching your focus quickly and without interruption between the various critical tasks involved in climbing a complete route.

Tip: Focus enhances the mind-body-rock connection and, thus, the odds of success. Commit a few weeks to actively train focus. After approximately ten focus-training sessions, you'll begin to feel more "connected" to the rock and more focused in the midst of stressful situations. Your performance will soar.

MAINTAINING CONTROL AND POISE

Emotional control in sports, also called "poise," is fundamental to optimal performance. Dealing with pressure before you climb (as discussed earlier) is a good start, but controlling emotion as you climb is just as important and often much more difficult. Ultimately, you must be able to rein in your emotions and react constructively to any errors or "surprises" as you climb, otherwise you'll forever be stuck climbing way below your true potential. It's natural for nervous energy and emotions to rise as you perform in a sport such as climbing— it happens to the very best. It's how you deal with it and how often you deal with it that makes the difference.

One effective approach is to break the climb into many small parts, each ending at a decent rest position. Memorize the exact rest locations and, if possible, the body position to be used at each of these "break points." (This is something you should add into your preclimb visualization ritual.) At these predetermined spots, you will "zero" your emotions and tensions and gather yourself for the next part of the climb. An effective method for doing this is the instant centering sequence (ICS) (see page 73).

ICS is a simple, effective means of maintaining complete control of your mind and body in the midst of a difficult climb. In centering, you deliberately direct your thoughts inward (and away from the climb for a moment) to check and adjust your breathing and level of muscular tensions and to counter any self-defeating thoughts. Scan your body for undesirable changes that have taken place since the last break point,

Poise, confidence and a good spotter always help. The author bouldering in Pennsylvania.

Photo: Mike McGill

things like rapid breathing, over-gripping holds, and tightening of antagonistic muscles. Make immediate corrections before the problem snowballs. Otherwise, you will become a "climber out of control" with an early and ugly end to your climbing guaranteed. Worse yet, no one will want to climb with you if you're spastic and spewing curses.

Practice ICS at home, the gym, or while climbing known routes. As with any skill, you need to practice regularly to become proficient in its use. Do so and in just a few weeks you'll be able to "center" yourself on any climb—anywhere and in just a few seconds.

Tip: Controlling emotions as you climb is tantamount to controlling your performance outcome. Break every climb into logical parts defined by rest positions. At these "break points," perform the instant centering sequence (ICS) to reset your emotions and renew your optimal performance state for next part of the climb.

Instant Centering Sequence

Perform ICS while at rest positions on a climb or in every day situations where you are upright and alert. At first, take a few minutes and go through the steps slowly. With practice you'll be able to "get centered" in a second or two.

1. Uninterrupted breathing: Continue your current breathing cycle, concentrating on smooth, deep, even breaths.

2. Positive face: Flash a smile regardless of your mental state. Research shows that a positive face "resets" the nervous system so it's less reactive to negative stress. You'll feel the difference immediately.

3. Balanced posture: Lift your head up, keep your shoulders loose, your back comfortably straight and abdomen free of tension. A balanced posture makes you feel light, with a sense of no effort in action. A tense, collapsed posture restricts breathing reduces blood flow, slows reaction time and magnifies negative feelings.

4. Wave of relaxation: In this step you perform a "tension check." Scan all your muscles in a quick sweep to locate unnecessary tension. Let go of those tensions, making your body calm with your mind remaining alert.

5. Mental check: Be focused, positive, and unhindered about the task at hand. Then send it!

SELF-TALK YOURSELF TO SUCCESS

Much of this chapter has been about increasing awareness of mind and body. Neither can be ignored, as they are inseparable and intimately affect each other. A simple example of this is that preclimb shakes can make you anxious, and anxiety can give you preclimb shakes. To combat this inside-out or outside-in self-destruction, you've been presented with several effective tools such as ICS, visualization, preclimb rituals, and focus training. This chapter concludes with one more powerful self-management tool: self-talk. Whether you are aware or not, this is something you undoubtedly do already to some degree. However, conscious use of self-talk is the goal, and it's paramount to maximizing performance.

We think in pictures and words. The pictures we "see" and the words we "say" are the seeds of reality. Earlier I discussed the importance of controlling the mental images and "making movies" via visualization. This last section is about tuning into the constant chatter of words in your head and how you can use it to affect reality as well. This is your self-talk.

Self-talk can affect sport success as much as training habits and technical skills. As an example, let's consider two climbers of equal fitness and skills, but vastly different self-talk. Before attempting the same climb, they each think to themselves:

CLIMBER A	CLIMBER B
"This route looks harsh."	"This route looks challenging."
"I hope I don't fall."	"I'll give it my best effort."
"I might be too short."	"Light weight is an advantage."
"It feels too hot to climb well."	"My muscles feel warm and strong."
"Many people are watching me."	"Focus on the process, not outcome."
"I feel nervous."	"I'm confident, centered, and ready."
"It might be too pumpy for me."	"I've trained hard, it looks doable."

Which climber do you think will have the better performance? Climber A is indulging in self-putdowns that plant the seeds of almost certain failure. Meanwhile Climber B is affirming his preparedness and considering the upside to the weather and his physique. Your goal is to emulate the positive approach of Climber B and ward off the negative psyche of Climber A. Let's look at both.

Negative self-talk is insidious because you may have been saying such things for so long that you're unaware of it or even think it's normal. Thus, becoming aware of all your self-talk at home, school, work, and while climbing is the first step. You must break down the negatives and rebuild them into valid positives. Beware that simply drowning yourself in false positives holds no value. For instance, if you're short, telling yourself "I'm tall" is a farce. Instead, counter with a valid reason why being short and light might be an advantage on the climb.

Effective self-talk is affirmation of your preparedness and positive attributes, not hopes or wishes of what you want to happen. Like Climber B, your self-talk should relate to positives in the reality of the given situation. Confirm why you should do well.

Many top athletes actively use self-talk as they perform to enhance focus, remind themselves of fundamental skills, and counter false-negative thoughts. When climbing, you might say to yourself, "relax grip," "focus on the feet," "keep breathing," "good rest ahead—hang in there," "get centered," "only one more hard move," "use straight-arm hangs," "climb faster," and so forth. But keep the affirmations (valid positives) going long after the climb is over, whether at home, work, the gym, or wherever. Like your muscles, your mental "state" is constantly in flux—either you're building it up or tearing it down. And always base your self-talk on what you have, not on what you don't have. In the long term, its influence on your climbing (and life) will be remarkable!

Tip: Positive self-talk enhances your overall mental state and the odds of success. Use self-talk to counter false negatives, remember skills, and reinforce your positive qualities. Use positive self-talk throughout the day and in all aspects of your life, as you can not just turn it on when you go climbing.

Lisa Ann Hörst on her
second 5.12 redpoint,
"Love Life" (5.12b),
Lancaster, Pennsylvania.

Climbing Your First 5.12 (& Beyond!)

CHAPTER 5

> *The best way to push yourself the hardest and do the most amazing things is by having fun—not going up on something because someone said it would be impressive, but because you can't imagine any other place on the planet you'd rather be.*
>
> —Peter Croft

Training on a steep home or commercial wall can be a blast, but nothing beats finding a beautiful route at some crag and on-sighting it—well, maybe falling in love with a rad-looking project, working it, training for it, dreaming of it, and then sending it does.... In any case, when reading a performance guidebook such as this one, it's easy to forget what this sport is all about—getting outside and climbing rock!

For many readers, the goal is to climb 5.12, while for others it may be 5.8 or 5.14. The numbers really don't matter; it's pushing your boundaries that counts. This gives you that "must-experience-it-to-understand-it" climber's high, and it builds character and confidence that carry over into all your other activities.

In this chapter, I'll touch on some of the basics relating to your performance at the crags from "picking a route" to "tricks for tough climbs." The meat of this chapter is strategic and tactical information for on-sighting routes and working redpoint projects. I do not cover issues of safety or belaying or the hundreds of specific movements and body-positioning skills. Consult *Advanced Rock Climbing, Sport Climbing* or *Clip n' Go* for specific instruction in these areas.

Consider that performing near your physical limit, whether on-sight or redpoint, is very "mental." Although I will discuss some tactical head games in this chapter, see Chapter 4 for comprehensive spray on this topic.

PICKING THE RIGHT ROUTE

Practice or Performance?

The type of route you choose depends on whether the day's goal is practice or performance. If skill practice is the goal, pick a route that works one of your known weaknesses. For instance, if you are intimidated or have technical difficulty on roof routes, pick a roof route to work (upon completing a few warm-up climbs, of course). Whatever your weakness, be it slabs, thin fingercracks, steep routes, or thin vert faces, it's your commitment to work them frequently that will make you better.

If performance is the goal du jour, exploit your strengths! Pick routes that focus on what you do well, "look good," and inspire. Exploiting your strengths won't make you better, but it will make for some brilliant ascents—the goal of performance days.

On-sight or Redpoint?

Your next decision is whether you'll climb on-sight or work a route for redpoint. If you've found a climb you like, the grade may determine this matter for you. It's unlikely you'll on-sight more than a letter above your hardest on-sight to date (although it can happen).

If you have a wide choice of suitable routes at "your grade," favor on-sight over redpoint at a 2 to 1 ratio. Both are valuable experiences, but on-sight climbing provides greater potential for learning. Overemphasis on redpointing is an all-too-common mistake of climbers "in search of big numbers." They spend a lot of the time flailing on the rock, learn very little and, only occasionally, succeed on such difficult routes. Exclusive use of this approach can demoralize and injure you, and has less learning and practice value than on-sighting routes near your limit.

Climber A has built a solid foundation for progressing into 5.12 with many ascents near his on-sight level.

Climber B has not consolidated his current on-sight level and will struggle to advance.

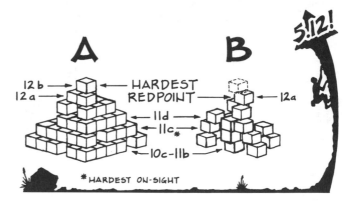

Consolidate Your Grade-Level Ability

Two common mistakes in cragging are: (1) working redpoint routes too hard for you, and (2) on-sighting routes too far below your limit. It's better to focus your climbing near your maximum ability level. Such "consolidation" of ability at a grade level establishes the foundation from which you can push the envelope just a bit farther.

Except for warm-up climbs, pick routes within one number grade of your hardest on-sight. For instance, if 5.11c is your top on-sight level, select routes between 5.10c and 5.11d to on-sight. Sending several routes at this grade solidifies your

John Blumenthal climbing for performance on "Apollo Reed" (5.13a), Summerville Lake, West Virginia.

Photo: Michael Miller

ability, while hiking a zillion 5.10a's or hoping to "get lucky" on a 5.13a holds little value.

As for picking a grade to redpoint, work routes between 5.11d and 5.12c, as per the example above. Routes in the low end of this range may go in just two or three tries while the hard lines may take several days. Avoid getting involved in projects more than a number grade beyond your best on-sight (no routes beyond 5.12c in this example). You'll use up too much time on too many climbing days when you could be consolidating your current ability level. The sooner you firm up skill and confidence at your current level, the faster you'll progress for real beyond it!

Use the four climbing grade pyramids located in the back of the book to plot your progress toward 5.12. Fill in the route name and date of each redpoint. Try to complete one row of blocks at a time; however, if you find just the right route don't hesitate to push on to the next level.

ON-SIGHT CLIMBING TIPS

Get Warmed and Primed

In a sense, on-sight climbing is like stepping into the ring with an unknown boxer. You don't know exactly what to expect until the fight's underway—you might get everything thrown at you right away or not until the end, and just when you feel you're in control, you get floored. Boxers know this and step into the ring only after performing a lengthy prefight warmup that has every cell of the body primed to the max. Your preparations for an on-sight should have a similar effect, of course, minus the profuse sweating of a prizefighter.

This lengthy comparison highlights an important fact—that many climbers fail on routes due to lack of proper warmup. The ubiquitous flash pump is evidence of this. A properly warmed muscle will not pump out prior to the maximal exertion levels you're accustomed to from training. If you start the day fresh and perform a lengthy warmup, you will never be surprised by an out-of-nowhere flash pump that sends you to the floor. Instead, you'll know pretty much where you are with respect to pumping out and be able to attack the route in a suitable fashion.

What's the best way to warm up for a serious on-sight attempt? Some full-body stretching and sports massage of the fingers and forearms is a good start, but lots of submaximal climbing mileage is the ticket. Begin two number grades below your hardest on-sight and do about four one-pitch routes, each a little harder than the last. If 5.11c is your on-sight limit, start with a 5.9, followed by a 5.10a, then a 5.10c, ending with an easy 5.11. Take a 20- to 60-minute rest, and you'll be ready and primed for a great on-sight attempt. Most importantly, experiment to find out what works best for you in different situations. For example, when traditional climbing you might only have time for two warmups, whereas at a sport crag you might send up to six half-rope clip-ups before getting on the "route of the day." No matter what your approach, avoid a vicious flash pump like Roseanne in a singles club.

Scoping the Route

You only get one chance to on-sight a route. Scope it out like there's no tomorrow—because there isn't!

Clearly, a route well below your limit doesn't require much scoping other than determining issues of gear, safety and maybe rest positions. But before you step onto a near-your-limit route, bag every bit of information available, as just one minor detail overlooked might tip the scales against you. Always view the route from at least three different perspectives, not just straight on as is common. Look for hidden holds in corners, around arêtes, above and below bulges or anywhere else they might hide. Next consider protection and clipping positions. Rack up your gear accordingly. Spend a lot of time determining every possible rest location and the best body position for each. Look for hand jams, knee locks, heel hooks, stems, and any small ledge you might be able to move laterally to reach. Of course, none of these rests are "for-sures" but at least you know the possibilities and can attack the route appropriately.

The most obvious scoping concern is the sequence itself. The more angles and views you can get, the better. Is there a boulder or tree you can climb for a unique angle? Is there an easy route nearby you can climb to get a fair side view of the route? Maybe use binoculars to search for minor details. As you decipher the "best-looking" sequence, keep an open mind for alternative possibilities. You may want to memorize two sequences through the apparent crux section, then make the choice in person when you get there. Finally, don't get stuck in the bottom-up paradigm when figuring sequences. Often you can unlock a puzzling sequence by mentally down climbing it from an obviously good hold or rest.

Your scope job may take anywhere from five minutes to an hour depending on the complexity of the route. (However, some persons will thoroughly scope and visualize a "significant" route for hours during a rest day.) Now that you've gathered all the data, it's time to preprogram a successful ascent with visualization.

Tips for "Reading" Route:

• Scope a route from at least three different perspectives looking for hidden holds, rest positions, gear placements, and the best sequence.

• Climb a nearby boulder, tree, or even a by-the-side climb to gain a novel view of the route. Consider using binoculars.

• Decipher two conceivable sequences to any uncertain-looking sections.

• Use reverse sequencing to help solve puzzling sections.

Preprogramming the Ascent

Making the most of the data you've gathered requires vivid "movie making" via visualization. I'm not talking about mental review of hold location and order as many persons incorrectly term visualization (what they're doing is simply mental rehearsal). Visualization, as used by top athletes around the world, is vivid, extremely detailed, multicolor mental movie making—we're talking Steven Spielberg—which, through repetition, preprograms future reality in the brain!

After scoping your route, but before roping up, find a quiet out-of-the-way spot to sit or lay down for a few minutes. Relax and clear your mind of all other concerns (maybe run quickly through the relaxation sequence provided in Chapter 4 on page 68). Begin recalling the images you "shot" earlier of the holds, location, order, rest, and gear. Blend them together into a moving picture. As you proceed, increase the brightness and detail of the movie to accentuate the preprogramming affect. (See page 63 in Chapter 4 for a complete discussion of visualization.)

Be careful not to program negatives or any uncertainty into your movies. If necessary, go back and rescope the climb to clarify the pictures or refigure a sequence. Then go back to your quiet spot and continue on with visualization.

Lower levels of arousal are ideal for thin, technical routes. Here Rick Mix is dancing up "The Nothing Atolls" (5.13a),at Bellefonte, Pennsylvania.

Optimizing Your Arousal

Arousal is your internal state of alertness or excitement. Your arousal is low when nodding off during your partner's pathetically slow leads and probably quite high when your last piece of gear pops out and slides down the rope. In climbing, arousal levels are in a constant state of flux, often determined by the pressure imposed by a given situation. As you react to each new situation, your awareness (or lack thereof) of changing arousal and your ability to control the arousal level has an enormous impact on your performance.

Ideal arousal levels in climbing relate to the physical and cognitive requirements of a route. The more complex the motor skills and sequence, the lower the optimal arousal level. For instance, a thin face climb demands pinpoint foot placements and complex sequencing, and thus is optimally performed in a calm, focused state. Oppositely, a short, steep route of burley moves between big, obvious holds is best performed with vim and vigor. Of course, most climbs fall somewhere between these extremes and are best performed with moderate levels of arousal.

Your task is to determine the ideal arousal level for the route you plan to on-sight, consciously preproduce that

arousal and then maintain it throughout the climb. Since most persons tend to be pretty psyched up before a "big" ascent, the most common situation is needing to moderate high arousal. Any thoughts that lower pressure or expectancy will help decrease arousal. Use the relaxation and centering sequences detailed in Chapter 4 to farther moderate arousal levels, the latter being your weapon of choice while climbing.

In case you need to increase arousal levels, start with some light physical activity to up your heart rate and blood pressure (like some jumping jacks or a brief jog along the base of the cliff). Next, make your preclimb visualization overly bright, exaggerated, and moving at higher-than-usual speed. As a last resort, stimulants such as caffeine increase arousal but also add to jitters and nervousness. In the end, it comes down to your awareness and experience in a wide range of situations and just "knowing" what's the right level for you.

High arousal is optimal for attacking powerful moves and short, steep routes. The author in Arco, Italy.

Photo: Mike McGill

Tips for Optimizing Arousal

• Determine the "best" level of arousal for each route. Create higher levels for powerful sequences and low to moderate arousal for the more technical and complex.

• Moderate arousal by lowering expectations and pressure—focus on the process not the possible outcome. Also, use the relaxation and centering sequences provided in chapter four.

• Increase arousal via additional warm-up exercises, bright "loud" visualization, and possibly caffeine.

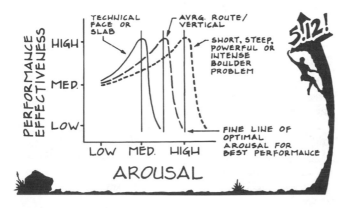

Tactics are Route Dependent

There is no "best" on-sight strategy. Always tailor your tactics to the route at hand. If it's a thin route with dicey pro you may need to "sample" the crux section by climbing up, then back down to a rest position (maybe several times), before trying it for real. On a powerful sport route the best strategy may be an all-out blitzkrieg of going immediately "with what looks right." Your typical approach will be somewhere between these extremes, although it's not uncommon to occasionally incorporate both on the same climb. As an example, you may be able to down-climb to the ground from an early crux, then after a rest, send it and the upper section with the blitzkrieg approach.

Your on-route rest tactics are very critical as well. Program the location of all rest spots during your preclimb visualization. However, don't hesitate to abandon a rest stance and move on, if you find it takes more effort than it's worth. Keep an open mind to other rest possibilities—whether a novel knee bar or manky handjam in a pocket. Even the slightest rest in the midst of a savage sequence just might save the day. Thus, the bottom line in on-sighting: be creative, ad-lib at will, and know when to rest and when to climb like a madman.

John Higgins taking it to the limit on "Hinterland" (5.12b)

Photo: Mike McGill

Taking It to the Limit

The most powerful piece of information as you attempt an on-sight is that the route goes! All the holds are there just waiting for you to unlock the order and physically put them together. A 100-percent belief that it can be climbed is tantamount to having it halfway in the bag.

A large percentage of would-be on-sighters fail because they never truly believe in a route. This is evident by their sloppy preclimb preparation or their namby-pamby effort ending in a "take" or "I'm falling." Oppositely, the best on-sight climbers know it goes, and believe they have what it

Final On-sight Tips

• Tailor your on-sight tactics to each route. Carefully "read" each climb and plan the best strategy based on your past experiences.

• Believe in the route! Even a fleeting doubt that it might not go is tantamount to adding a 10-pound weight to your back.

• Leave nothing on the "table." You only get one chance to on-sight a route—so fall trying not quitting.

takes to do it, too. They plan meticulously, climb aggressively, and fall only rarely. And when they do fall, it's often sudden and with great surprise—surely they didn't expect to fall, they expected to flash!

So assuming the route is well protected and you have an alert belayer, always take your on-sight attempts to the limit. Use all the strategy and skill you have, put the pedal to the metal and empty the tank. Do this, and you'll "win" quite frequently, leaving fewer vendetta projects to come back to and redpoint.

WORKING A REDPOINT ROUTE

Get Data Rich

Compared to the tight "rules" of on-sight climbing, working a redpoint is a veritable free-for-all of data-gathering and on-route tactics. The need for extensive preclimb scoping is much less because you get first hand information as you "work" the route. Remember, in redpointing, the rope is a tool. Hanging and falling are a means to the end, while in on-sight climbing it is the end.

Before beginning work on the project, gather information from other climbers who have worked-on or done the route. Don't worry about exact sequences yet, you may need or figure a different way anyhow. Instead, focus on the basics of gear, rests, where the crux(es) is (are) located and whether there are any hidden or "thank-God" holds. If there's no such beta available, take your best guess at it, then caste off up the route.

Your first goal is to hangdog up the entire route. The rope, gear, and your belayer are all fair tools to get you there. In fact, liberal use of the rope is advised to save vital energy you'll need later.

Chunking Down the Route

The benefits of chunking down a difficult climb into parts are both mental and physical. Psychologically, it reduces the burden of a long hard route by allowing you to consider its parts as several shorter, doable climbs. Physically, chunking lets you dedicate full energy to solving the crux chunk first, as if it were a route of its own. Only when this is sent, do you begin work on other "easier" parts of the climb.

Before you can chunk down the route, you need first-hand knowledge. Take a quick "reconnaissance run" up the climb to determine its logical parts—how you chunk down is, of course, route dependent. For instance, a route made up of 70 feet of moderate climbing followed by just 10 hard feet to the top is best chunked in two parts. Knowing the first 70 feet is doable, get to work on solving and linking the last 10 feet while you're fresh. On a climb with multiple cruxes, chunk down each difficult section into a "route" of its own defined by good rest positions first and gear placements second. Sport

Jim Taylor redpointing "Jesus and Tequila" (5.12b), New River Gorge, West Virginia.

Photo: Carl Samples

climbers commonly break down routes bolt by bolt (such as, a 10-bolt climb having 10 chunks). After the first "run" through the route, grade each part (such as, hardest, second-hardest, easiest, and so forth) in your mind considering that the upper parts may seem harder on redpoint due to fatigue. Always make solving the hardest part top priority.

Linking Chunks

The most popular method of "linkage" is to climb ever-increasing lengths of the route to the top. Consider the common scenario of working a route with the rope already through the top anchors. From the anchors, lower down the route (backclip if overhanging) only as far as you think you can "redpoint" back to the top. This might be only a 10-foot chunk if the end is the crux. If you succeed at that chunk, lower down and add another chunk to the linkup. Continue adding chunks until your starting point hits "easy ground" or the ground. This process of linking chucks can take hours or days depending on the length and difficulty of your project. But there's much greater value in this approach compared to the old start-from-the-ground method.

Linking from top down makes you extremely familiar and confident in the final portion. On redpoint, it's here you want to be especially dialed in due to the accumulation of mental and physical fatigue. Oppositely, the from-the-ground approach commonly leaves the climber thrashing to refigure the top part, which he has practiced much less. Such ground-up efforts are more likely to result in a fall off the final moves, making a waste of even the most heroic effort.

Interlace Physical and Mental Practice

As you work chunks and begin linkage, incorporate extensive visualization into the process. After each fall, review and visualize the correct sequence. Use your rest time between tries to run some mental movies of the route. On multiday efforts, use visualization on rest days to aid memory of and further code the desired sequence. Prepare a beta "map" of long, complex routes to help guide your visualization.

This crib sheet should contain all hand and foot holds, rest positions, shake outs, clips, or anything else that is a "must" to send the crux sequence. Number the order the holds are used, always specifying whether it's a left or right and hand or foot placement. Write down descriptive words or "names" for critical holds to add detail and accuracy to your visualization. Tips like "sloping edge—get off of it fast" or "pistol-grip hold—good for a quick chalk-up" really make things click on redpoint.

Build a Simulator

On a "big" project, use your beta map to build a simulator of the crux section on a home wall or at a local gym. Many top climbers do this to train for projects, especially during the off-season. An accurately built simulator develops motor skills and strength specific to the project, maintains move memory, and builds confidence.

Simulator training dates back at least to 1960 as John Gill began training for the small, pebbly Thimble route in the Needles of South Dakota. To simulate the difficult pebble pinching, Gill climbed the wall of a gymnasium by pinching nuts and bolts sticking out from the wall! Famous Colorado climber, Jim Collins used route simulators to train for Psycho roof and Genesis, and Tony Yaniro has been using simulator training for years, in preparation for his many cutting-edge ascents. As you've learned in this book, specificity of training is everything, and route simulators are as specific as training gets. Consider building a simulator of your next serious project.

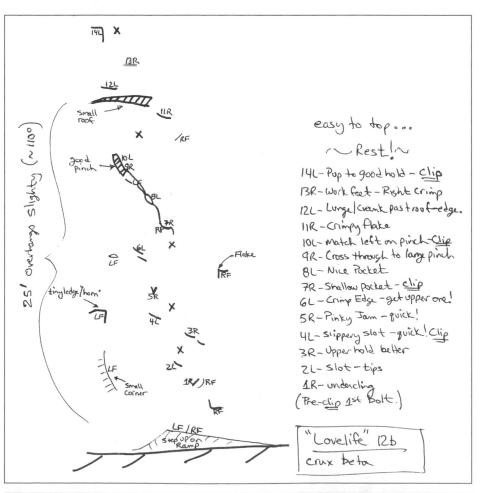

easy to top...

~ Rest!~

14L – Pop to good hold – clip
13R – Work feet – Right crimp
12L – Lunge/Crank past roof edge.
11R – Crimpy flake
10L – Match left on pinch–clip
9R – Cross through to large pinch
8L – Nice Pocket
7R – Shallow Pocket – clip
6L – Crimp Edge – get upper one!
5R – Pinky Jam – quick!
4L – Slippery slot – quick! Clip
3R – Upper hold better
2L – Slot – tips
1R – undercling
(Pre-clip 1st Bolt.)

"Lovelife" 12b
crux beta

Rest Long and Prosper

By nature, redpointing a route at the far reaches of your ability demands perfection. To maximize the odds of success, you need to be healthy, confident, well rested, and well warmed up. For a same-day attempt, take a double- to triple-length rest—whereas you normally rest about 30 minutes between efforts, take at least 90 minutes before you go for the redpoint.

On a multiday worked route, take at least two rest days before attempting the redpoint. On the big day, get to the crag early and perform a long, gradual warmup. You need to be mentally and physically primed to peak efficiency to send the route. This may mean several hours of warmup climbing, stretching, and additional visualization. Kurt Smith tells how before redpointing his major project Slice of Life (5.13d) he sent as many as six routes in the 5.11 and 5.12 range. These were obviously climbs he had wired, but sending all six with ease prepared his mind and body for the big brawl.

Finally, for long-term projects worked over many weeks (possibly via simulator training), schedule the redpoint for the week following the end of a 10-week training cycle. (Remember, week ten is a full week off after the savage maximum strength and anaerobic endurance phases.) Upon completing this rest week, you will be stronger and more focused than at any time in the previous few weeks—the perfect time to redpoint your "hardest-ever" project.

Final Thoughts

Okay, you've worked it, visualized it and linked all the hard parts. You are well-rested, warmed, and primed like never before. Success or failure may now come down to your final thoughts as you step onto the rock. That's right, just like a prizefighter stepping into the ring, you must believe 100 percent or else you're going down. Attempting a climb at your limit leaves no room for cruel doubts that will ultimately leave you hanging (on the rope).

Tune into your final thoughts after gearing up (shoes, harness, and so forth) and being put on belay. Close your eyes, take a few deep breaths and relax throughout your body. Now visualize successful execution of the route one final time. End this mental movie with the vision of successfully reaching the anchors, ledge, or cliff top, then open your eyes and crank it!

One Chunk at a Time

As you begin climbing, take the route one chunk at a time whether that's bolt to bolt or rest to rest. (The burden of looking up and considering the route as a whole can be too great and may plant the seeds of failure in the form of jitters and doubts.) Mentally tick off each chunk as you complete it—this confidence builder will help propel you upward. Momentum

Tips for working a redpoint

• Obtain as much beta as possible from other climbers who have done the route. Inquire about gear, rest locations, hard-to-find holds and where the hardest parts of the route are located.

• Begin with a reconnaissance run up the climb. Use the rope freely as hangdogging conserves energy. Learn the basics of the route and identify where the hard, moderate and easy parts are located.

• Chunk down the route into "believable" parts. This is important as a long, hard route carries a heavy burden when considered as a whole. Begin serious work on the hardest part first, then work the other chunks ending with the easiest section.

• Linkage of the route should be done top down. For instance, link the last 20 feet to the top, if successful, rest and try to link the last 40 feet, and so on.

• Use visualization between attempts and on rest days. Prepare a beta map of complex sequences to guide accurate visualization.

• Build an indoor simulator for serious, long-haul projects. Set a modular-hold copy of the crux sequence for the most specific training available other than the route itself.

will crescendo as you reach the upper part of the route, helping push you upward in the midst of increasing fatigue.

Living With Error (or air!)

Some redpoint projects go "easily," as you live out your mental movie and perform in the "zone." Other times you make mid-route errors such as botching a sequence—and maybe take air as the redpoint attempt comes to an abrupt end. No big deal! Remind yourself this is redpoint climbing not on-sight. The rules are different, and errors and failures are part of the learning process.

Let's consider the case of a mid-route error. You need to make a quick, often intuitive, call whether the error is a "fatal" or something you can live with and climb through. An example of a fatal error is botching a hand sequence which leaves you with an impossible reach. In this case, drop onto the rope to conserve energy for another attempt. However, before lowering to the ground, do the botched sequence one more time on toprope. Never start in the middle of a sequence (such as, at the botched move) but instead begin from the last break point and send the whole chunk. After doing this, visualize the correct sequence, and run the movie a few more times as you rest on the ground.

Minor mid-route errors are best accepted and "dropped to the ground." Say, your foot pops off a hold or you start to reach up with the wrong hand on a critical move. Instead of cursing the mistake, simply accept it as a sign to increase your focus then forget about it. To carry any thought of past errors is akin to carrying extra weight up the route.

The 110 Percent Solution

As in on-sight climbing, you cannot hold anything back when attempting a redpoint. Since the climb is at or beyond your known limits, 90 percent effort will not be enough. Throw everything you have at the rock—all your skill, experience, strength as well as any tricks you are armed with. Hanging on the rope thinking "I could have tried harder" is a real bummer.

Tips for redpointing your project:

• **Don't rush into a redpoint attempt. Put in necessary "work" duty then rest a lot. For a same-day redpoint try, triple your normal rest time between attempts. Consider taking a few rest days before going for the hardest projects.**

• **Final thoughts are key. Visualize a successful ascent of the entire route. Step onto the rock confident, relaxed, and ready to enter the zone.**

• **Attack the route one chunk at a time, as if ticking off several doable boulder problems. Focus on the process of climbing each chunk and forget about the ultimate outcome.**

• **Learn to live with your mistakes. "Climb through" minor errors in sequence and forget about them immediately. If you commit a "fatal error," hang on the rope, and figure out what went wrong. Reclimb the problem chunk, then lower to the ground, rest, and visualize the correct solution.**

• **Hold nothing back. Redpointing is about absolute perfection and absolute "go for it!"**

TRICKS FOR TOUGH CLIMBS

Whether redpoint or on-sight, it's often the clever fellows who pull off the brilliant ascents. Not clever as in cheating without anyone knowing it, but clever in the sense of finding a hidden hold or new rest, or use of special tactics on a given route. There is a myriad of "trick" moves I could cover from the "figure-4 lock-off" to the "elbow-knee bar lock." But as emphasized throughout, this book is not about teaching specific moves or techniques—personal one-on-one instruction is best for this—but instead presenting cutting-edge theories, principles, and strategies needed to pursue 5.12 and beyond.

All of Chapter 5 fits into the strategies category. This final section goes under the subhead of "trick" or "clever" strategies needed for the most insidious and continuous climbs.

Vary Grip Positions

The forearm muscles are almost always the critical point of failure when climbing at your limit. Thus, any trick you can use to extend their life should be exploited. One of the best tricks is conscious cycling of grip position while climbing. This distributes accumulating stress over a wide range of muscular motor units.

Back in Chapter 4, I explained how repeated use of the exact same grip position speeds up muscular failure. There is high training value in this approach (this is one reason HIT is so effective), but in "operational" situations, like redpointing, it's the kiss of death. Instead of rapid muscular failure, you want long-lasting performance like the Energizer rabbit. Constant variation of grip use does just that—it keeps you going and going and going….

Ultimately, each route dictates how far you can go with this strategy. For instance, a thin edgy Smith Rocks' route may limit you to cycling between crimp, open-hand, and an occasional "thumb-lock" grip. A pocketed Wild Iris route may allow use of all two- and three-finger "teams," as well as some thumb presses and a jam or two in large pockets.

Finally, if your project requires several powerful open-hand pulls near the end of the route, avoid this grip down low in favor of the crimp grip. Thanks to specificity of grip strength, overuse of one grip position early on conserves contact strength in other positions for use later in the climb.

Focus on the Feet

"When the times get tough, focus on the feet." Remind yourself of this every time you begin to struggle on a route! Due to the proximity of the eyes to the hands, it's quite natural to overfocus on hand positioning at the expense of finding the best foot holds. Ironically, the key to unlocking many routes lies in effective use of the feet. Consider how often you have fallen, only to notice a killer foot placement you missed.

Increasing focus on the feet takes practice and self-awareness. For starters, ask your belayer to yell at you to "look for feet" as you begin having difficulties on a route. The same thing goes in the gym or while bouldering. The more your attention is redirected toward finding the best foot holds, the more automatic it will become in the future.

On difficult routes, some climbers place small chalk "tickmarks" just above critical foot holds as visual cues. This practice is quite effective when climbing fast is essential—still,

Trick moves such as Brett Spencer-Green's heel-and-toe lock here on "Vitamin H" can make some 'impossible' moves doable, and some hard moves easy!

Photo: Stewart Green

you need to remember to look down in the first place! Consult Chapter 4 to learn how to train for increased foot focus.

Climb Faster, Not Slower

Climbing too slow is one of the biggest errors in redpointing. Unlike on-sight, you know where all the holds, rests, and gear are located, so little time and thought needs to be spent on these issues. In fact, when redpointing you should climb as fast as possible without making technical errors.

Energy expenditure in climbing is proportional to time—it's like the longer Motel 6 "leaves the light on," the higher their electric bill. Since you have a finite amount of energy to send a route, it makes sense to get on and off small holds and through the crux sequence as fast as possible. Of course, blow a sequence by climbing sloppily and the energy issue is moot.

Cool your engines at the predetermined rest positions, then shift back into high gear as you climb into the next difficult section. Indeed this goes against conventional wisdom that says "proceed carefully in difficult times." While you might heed this "wisdom" on some on-sight or traditional routes, ignore it and climb faster on well-protected redpoint attempts.

Recover Faster with the G-Tox

The typical "rest" or "breakpoint" on a redpoint is not a comfy stance you can camp out on forever. More common, it's an okay hand hold (you can match hands on it, if you're lucky) combined with a foot or lower-body position that takes significant weight off the arms. A few seconds to a couple minutes later, the "rest" may become an energy drain as it begins to take more energy to remain there than you recover. A smart climber is "out-of-there" by this point of diminishing returns.

Knowing when you've reached this critical point comes from experience redpointing and anaerobic-endurance "interval" training. Assuming you know how long to stay at a rest, the goal becomes doing anything to maximize recovery (detoxing the forearms is the main concern) during the respite. The normal protocol for recovery at marginal mid-climb rests is relaxed breathing and "shaking out" the arms. As we all know, this yields noticeable recovery. However, you can foster even greater recovery through use of the "G-tox."

The "G-tox" is only slightly different from the shakeout described above—you alternate the position of the "shake-out" arm between the normal "down" position and a "raise-hand" position (like in school). The regimen I find works best is 5 to 10 seconds with the arm above your head, followed by 5 to 10 seconds in the down position. Keep repeating until you sense you're near the point of diminishing returns, then get climbing.

My G-tox method works a bit better than the normal shakeout by using gravity to its advantage. During use of the "normal" hands-down shakeout, blood pools in the forearms (the "pump") partially due to gravity's hindrance of venous return flow toward the heart. Addition of the raised-hand position uses gravity to enhance venous return of "used" blood out of the arm. This return flow takes some lactic acid with it, and allows more fresh, oxygenated blood to enter. The end result is greater recovery in the same amount of time as the old standard method. (How much extra is hard to say, but even a modest 5 or 10 percent extra is significant when climbing at your limit.) Britain's On the Edge magazine recently reported that Robyn Erbesfield is now using the G-tox. It is time for you to give it a try.

Boone Speed detoxing in the midst of "Malvado" at American Fork, Utah.

You can speed mid-route recovery by using the G-Tox at such rests. Alternate the position of your resting arm between the down position (pictured) and a raised-hand position.

Photo: Stewart Green

Tips on tricks:

• Cycle your grip over the widest range of possible positions to spread out fatigue. Or if you know you need "full power" of a specific grip for the crux, avoid its use up to that point.

• When the going gets tough, focus on the feet. Of course, try to pay constant attention to finding the best footholds as the legs are stronger than the arms.

• Climb faster, not slower, through difficult sequences to conserve energy.

• Use the G-tox to enhance recovery on those all-too-brief marginal shakeouts. Alternate your resting arm between the raised-hand and dangling-by-the-side position, shaking it slightly for 5 to 10 seconds in each position. Repeat this process as long as the rest stance allows.

The author on "Je Suis
un Légende" (7a+),
Verdon Gorge, France.

Photo: Stewart Green

Frequently Asked Questions

All that you throw at the rock comes back into yourself. You become the result of your struggles, the sum of your efforts.
　　　　　　　—Todd Skinner

One of my favorite winter activities (besides training in my home gym!) is conducting Peak Performance Rock Climbing seminars. Since I can only cover the tip of the training-for-climbing iceberg during the two-hour sessions, each inevitably ends with an enthusiastic, often lengthy, question-and-answer period. Interestingly, I hear a lot of the same questions from attendees at various gyms. Since you, too, may have pondered similar thoughts, I decided to finish the book with some of the more important and interesting questions and answers on subjects not addressed earlier.

Feel free to drop me a question of your own. Make it as specific as possible and I'll try to return a brief answer via e-mail or snail. Also, give me the okay and I may even use it in a future publication.

Q. It seems that most people doing routes 5.12 and harder climb full-time. Although I've been climbing less than a year, I desperately want to crank at that level. Do I need to quit my job, sell my house, and become a climbing "bum" to make the grade?

Keep your job and house, and put in a few more years of regular climbing and focused training. Chances are 5.12 and 5.13 are within your reach without a major upheaval in your life.

Thousands of people climb 5.12 and have a "normal" life. I know of a couple teachers, a restaurant manager, several lawyers, a salesman, a contractor, two doctors, even a librarian who regularly climb 5.12s as weekend warriors. The key ingredients common in all these individuals are a dedication to train hard a couple days each week after work and a willingness to travel many weekends to pulldown on good rock.

The weekday training must be specific to climbing—forget the local health club. Join a climbing gym or, better yet, build a home wall. A small, steep home wall makes a good workout possible on even the most hectic days. An hour of bouldering on an overhanging wall trains the strength, endurance and many of the techniques you'll need in your quest for the twelfth grade.

Rick Thompson works 40+ hours a week as the Access Fund's Land Acquisitions Director. He also redpoints 5.12. Here he is on the "Little Shaver's Club" (5.12b).

Photo: Carl Samples

On weekends, travel, travel, travel. It's important to get experience on many different kinds of rock, so don't lock into spending every weekend at the same (closest) crag. Dedicate Saturday to working on a couple project routes, then climb for mileage (practice) on Sunday.

Finally, long-term gains require consistent and congruent actions. Plan your workout and travel schedule as far into the future as possible—ad lib workouts won't cut it. Neither will activities that run counter to the nine absolutes (see Chapter 1), albeit excessive training or partying. Your climbing will suffer and you'll come up short of your goals.

So for now, stay the course. Train smart, climb hard, and drop me a note when you send your first 5.12!

Q. While on a road trip, how many days per week can I climb without seeing a major drop off in performance or risking overuse injury?

Four days climbing per week is a good number for planning purposes; however, adjust the actual number according to amount of sleep, quality of nutrition, and intensity of climbing. Assuming reasonable sleep and diet habits, the number of rest days should be in direct proportion to the intensity of your climbing.

High-end climbers such as Todd Skinner frequently take two or three days off after a single day of maximal effort on a cutting-edge project. Extreme efforts require extreme recovery. If attempting (or training for) a severe redpoint, you might climb as little as twice a week while resting five days.

More typical of a road trip is the desire to pack in lots of climbing near or just below your limit. When I'm on trips, I place greater value on sending lots of 5.12s as opposed to spending a week on a single super-hard project. Many others agree on this approach making the two days on, one day off, two days on, two days off schedule quite popular. Here, you'll get in four good days of climbing per week along with enough rest to help prevent overuse injuries and maintain performances level.

When alpine or big-wall climbing, you may be able to survive on just one or two rest days per week. By today's cragging standards, many alpine routes are quite "moderate" making for a workout higher in volume than intensity. Similarly, mixed climbing on big walls involves lots of "hanging around" and "easy" free climbing. Of course, there are other variables that can complicate matters in these settings such as lack of food and water, high altitude, and poor weather. Ultimately, awareness of the situation and yourself must dictate the schedule.

As a final note, when sport climbing it's best to avoid

climbing more than two consecutive days. Repeating the same stressful moves and sequences—as in working a route—is especially hard on the tendons, muscles, and nervous system. Three or more straight days of this type of climbing will eventually lead to a decline in performance and possibly injury. Use an every-other-day climbing schedule or the two-on, one-off, two-on, two-off schedule presented above.

Tip: Take rest days in proportion to the intensity of your climbing. Two days rest per week may suffice when climbing moderate alpine or big wall routes. Peak performance on high-end climbs may require two or three days off per single day of high-intensity climbing. As a rule, avoid cragging more than two consecutive days.

Q. Is it true that indoor climbing can hurt outdoor, real-rock performance?

Yes and no! To explain my answer, let's consider the pros and cons of indoor climbing. First the pros, which clearly outweigh the cons. Indoor walls bring climbing closer to where we live, allowing for more regular practice of skills. Bouldering caves and home walls offer excellent sport-specific training for the fingers and forearms. Artificial walls can (and have) given birth to new moves that are also useful on real rock climbing. And pulling down indoors is a fun, rainy day alternative to climbing outside (important in the East!).

Now, the main drawback of indoor walls—they are a poor representation of real rock. Period. While most of the moves and techniques are the same as used outdoors, the holds, texture, and terrain are very different. This greatly limits transfer of skill from manmade to real rock and hence the "yes" portion of my answer. Excessive indoor climbing commonly leads to lackluster footwork at the crags. Real rock foot holds are harder to spot and use, and their frictional properties are less predictable. In addition, no indoor wall can prepare you for the variety of techniques you'll need to excel outside.

Don't get me wrong; I'm a huge advocate of indoor walls. Commercial and home walls have great strength-training value. However, if real-rock climbing is your goal, you must get out on the real stuff regularly to maintain your form and technique and gain "real world" experience.

Tip: Use indoor walls as a supplement to outdoor climbing—not the reverse. For optimal results, combine indoor bouldering to build strength and high-mileage days on real rock to train endurance and technique.

"Rising star" Katie Brown excels by mixing it up–she climbs outdoors on weekends and trains at her local gym during the week.

Photo: Stewart Green

Q. There are no crags or climbing gyms nearby, nor do I have space to build a home wall. I've decided to buy a fingerboard and I'm wondering what type of training is best?

Use your fingerboard mainly to train maximum grip strength. Two brief, high-intensity workouts per week will improve finger strength with minimal risk of injury. But don't become overzealous and train too long or often—this almost guarantees injury. Here's a blueprint for a safe, effective workout.

Brief, high intensity hangs on a fingerboard develop finger strength. Here weight has been added in a fanny pack to increase the difficulty of hanging on a sloping hold.

Perform your fingerboard training according to the four "requirements" for effective maximum finger strength training as discussed in Chapter 3. Let's recap the four training requirements: (1) train at maximum intensity throughout the set, (2) produce muscular failure in less than one minute, (3) use movements and body positions specific to climbing, and (4) focus on and "fry" a single-grip position for an entire set. Well-designed fingerboard workouts can meet three of these four requirements. Still, you'll come up short in the category of "movements and positions specific to climbing." Oh well, let's make the most of it. Here's how:

Begin with a slow warmup of at least 15 minutes. A few minutes of light aerobic activity (such as jogging or jumping rope) is ideal but not mandatory; however, comprehensive stretching of the upper body is (see Chapter 3). Alternate stretching with a few sets of pull-ups on large holds. Finish up with some self massage of the fingers and forearms. The meat of your max finger-strength training should be a series of "repeaters." Keep your arms nearly straight and favor small- to medium-sized, reasonably comfortable holds. Avoid tweaky, sharp holds like the local sandbagger, and reserve the one-finger pockets until you reach 5.12 (you'll have something to look forward to!).

"Repeaters" involve six, maximum-intensity hangs on the same pair of holds. Each hang must last only 3 to 10 seconds followed by a rest of exactly 5 seconds. The whole set takes just over a minute. Now take a one-minute rest before beginning one more set on the same pair of holds. Rest again for one more minute, then move on to another set of holds. Work your "problem grips" first (for me pinches), then progress from smaller to larger holds as you tire. Beginners should work only six grips (twelve sets of repeaters), whereas advanced people can work ten grips for a total of 20 sets. Finally, it's important to add weight to your body when working any fingerboard grips on which you can hang for more than 10 seconds. Start with 5 pounds added to your harness and increase the weight gradually over several weeks. Another method for adding weight (which I prefer) is placing 2-pound divers weights in a fanny pack. This way you can add or subtract weight quickly between sets and in smaller 2-pound increments.

Q. Do vitamin and herbal supplements really enhance performance and promote "well-being"?

No vitamin or herbal supplements enhance performance anywhere near as much as a solid training and climbing program combined with quality rest and nutrition. Unless you're doing all these things right, invest your money in climbing trips or the stock market—you'll get better performance either way. However, if you are training according to the absolutes and principles discussed earlier, you may benefit from the handful of supplements that are both proven to work and legal. If that's you, here's what to consider when you go shopping.

Start by reminding yourself that most of what vitamin and herbal companies tell you are lies and half-truths. Sure, the ads are compelling, but the vast majority of supplements don't have a shred of evidence to back up the grandiose claims. What's more, ignore the testimonials of famous athletes (who have genetics and years of training to thank for their success) that are merely anecdotal and carry no scientific weight. Look for products proven effective in double-blind, placebo-controlled studies (and results published in peer-review journal). Here are a few such supplements proven useful for serious athletes. You'll need to decide for yourself whether they're worth your money.

More than 100 studies have shown that antioxidants prevent muscle damage and shorten recovery time. Although a half dozen different antioxidants work toward this end, I suggest vitamins C and E and selenium as they are synergistic and quite affordable. Buy the cheapest (generic) brands you can find, since when it comes to these vitamins they are all basically the same. As for "how much to take," total daily supplementation of 2.0 grams of vitamin C, 400 IU of vitamin E, and 100 mcg of selenium split into two doses (morning and evening) will suffice. However, individuals training at extremely high intensities and volumes can safely double these amounts.

Next, consider supplementing your protein intake. If you are not consuming enough protein, your body may be cannibalizing muscle, especially during long workouts or days of climbing. As with the antioxidants above, the Recommended Daily Allowance (RDA) for protein is far too low for hard-training athletes. Numerous studies have shown the need for between 1.0 and 1.5 grams of protein per kilogram body-weight per day to maintain positive nitrogen balance in athletes. For a 150-pound climber, this translates to between 70 and 100 grams per day—surely a difficult amount to eat without loading up on fattening dairy products and meat. Enter protein powder mixes.

Until a few years ago, many beverage mixes contained low-quality soy protein and were packed with carbohydrates. Much has changed since then. Several leading brands (available at General Nutrition Center stores or by mail order) now use high-quality whey protein with little accompanying carbohydrates. Specifically look for brands containing "lactose-free whey peptides." (Thank French researchers for showing the value of whey peptides.) This form of protein maintains nitrogen balance longer and possesses higher Biological Value than lean meat, chicken, fish, milk, or any other protein source! Hence, a glass of whey protein in the morning, after workouts, and before bed gives your body what it needs to rebuild, stronger, faster.

Then there's the latest rage in mainstream and athletic nutrition—herbal supplements. Unfortunately, most herbal products have a traditional basis that is hardly scientific. Many of today's herbal "nutritionists" sound more like modern-day snake oil salesman with their hocus-pocus claims of cures and effects. As always, there are a few exceptions.

Ma Huang (ephedra herb) is an effective central nervous system stimulant with effects similar to caffeine. Use it in moderation to help pump up workout intensity. Standardized ginseng (Ginsana is one popular brand name) enhances athletic performance (slightly) by improving the body's use of oxygen. Other "adaptogens" enthusiastically researched in Russia are now available in the United States. PrimeQuest is one such company whose herbal products contain adaptogens. Although the Russian research may not be up to U.S. standards, it seems safe to at least try the products. You can then decide for yourself if the results are worth the cost.

Tip: Purchase only supplements proven to benefit athletic performance in double-blind, placebo-control studies. When in doubt, save your money. Unless you're doing everything else right, you probably won't notice the effects anyway.

Q. I overheard a couple climbers talking about a new scale for classifying the energy release of different foods; I believe it's called the glycemic index. What is this index and of what use is it to climbers?

Consumption of high-glycemic index foods causes a rapid increase in blood sugar and then a large insulin response. Low-glycemic index foods produce more subtle variations. Climbers can use knowledge of the glycemic index to control energy levels and to speed recovery after a workout. Here's how.

Stable insulin levels are optimal for long-duration activities such as climbing, hiking, and long training sessions. Experts also agree that a steady insulin curve promotes muscle growth and discourages fat storage. This makes low- to medium-index foods preferred for climbers. High glycemic index foods produce large swings in blood sugar and an insulin "spike." One minute you are jonesing to crank another hard route and the next you're in the tank and ready to call it a day.

Figuring the glycemic index of certain foods is more difficult than it might seem at first. For instance, most foods classified as simple carbohydrates (cereal, candy, some fruit juices) are high-index foods. However, so are potatoes, white rice, bread, and bagels—all considered complex carbohydrates. Low glycemic index foods include vegetables, whole grains, brown rice, and milk (see table). As a general rule, the more processed and easily digestible a food, the higher its glycemic index (for example, liquids have higher index than similar food solids). High-fiber foods tend to elicit a slow insulin response and are low index. Finally, foods containing some protein and fat along with carbohydrates come in lower on the scale, too.

This last piece of information is useful if you don't have the gumption to memorize and use this index. Consuming some protein and fat during each of your carbohydrate feedings serves to moderate the overall glycemic response of the meal. So, for a long day at the crags, pack energy bars that contain a several grams of protein and fat, in addition to the carbohydrates (like PowerBars).

The one good time to consume high-glycemic index foods such as candy, juice, or pop is at the end of your workout or day of climbing. Intense exercise primes the muscles to immediately reload energy reserves in the form of glycogen. High blood sugar and the insulin spike help drive this repletion process. The optimal "window" for these high GI foods is the first two hours following exercise. After that, favor low- to medium-index foods for slow, steady refueling.

Tip: Choose low- to medium-glycemic index foods as the foundation of your diet to provide sustained energy throughout the day. Only consume high-index foods immediately after training and climbing to help speed repletion of energy stores.

Q. Is it necessary to take time off from climbing? I know a few people who break from climbing for a month or more claiming it helps their performance! Wouldn't climbing year-round maximize technical and physical gains?

No, climbing year-round is not a good practice; and yes, a month off can help your climbing! I qualify this answer by adding that this applies to persons who climb at least twice per week, consistently throughout the year.

The grind of climbing several days per week over the long term takes a mental and physical toll. After a few consecutive training cycles or a long road trip, motivation and performance are often flat or declining. Worse yet, trying to break the plateau by training harder (as per conventional wisdom)

Glycemic Index	
Foods	**GI**
peanuts	10
soybeans	15
fructose	20
broccoli	25
lentils	25
grapefruit	30
kidney beans	31
yogurt	32
milk	~35
ice cream	35
apples	36
beans (canned)	40
oranges	40
grapes	44
buckwheat pancakes	45
oatmeal	48
sweet potatoes	48
peas (frozen)	53
pastas	~55
brown rice	60
candy bars	~60
whole wheat bread	64
bananas	65
shredded wheat	65
raisins	68
white potatoes	70
white rice	70
corn chips	~70
rice cakes	~75
corn	75
white bread	76
cereal (most)	~80
honey	87
carrots	90
glucose	100

will produce even greater negative effects. Some time off is the fastest way back on track.

One month totally away from climbing—no gym climbing, no home walls, no thinking about climbing—during the off-season can yield great results. Sure, you'll lose a few percentage points of your strength, but that returns in a week or two when you start climbing again. What's important is that your renewed motivation may exceed previous levels giving birth to greater training and performance than ever before!

Physically, this downtime benefits you in two ways. First, it will nip in the bud any nagging or underlying injuries. Several weeks off and your tendons will surely be stronger than before, making them more resistant to injury as you return to pursue even higher grades. Your muscles also rebound as they finally get an extended recovery break. Accumulated fatigue from several training cycles may unknowingly have you on the verge of overtraining. If that's you, expect your maximum strength to actually increase a bit after three or four weeks rest from the "use and abuse."

The second benefit of occasional time off is a fascinating phenomenon called reminiscence. This long-known principle is based on the fact that your body remembers more about complex skills (call it muscle memory) than your conscious mind. Long bouts of regular climbing can leave you trying too hard, overanalyzing situations, and possibly too outcome-oriented. Your climbing movements may begin feeling awkward and forced, and your performance curve may be straightlining. Eventually, you'll be wondering, "Why isn't all this practice time making me better?"

Time away from climbing will clear your head, reduce expectations, and "reset" your intuitive sense of movement. Greeting your return to the rock will be more automatic and natural movement as your body remembers (reminisces) the well-learned motor skills of climbing. This "try softer" style will not overpower your body's "knowledge" of the skills as did the old "try-harder" approach. You'll be pleasantly surprised to find yourself climbing better, more efficiently, and with more "flow" than before. This powerful reminiscence effect has been experienced time and time again by participants in many sports ranging from golf to gymnastics. So, next time your climbing stagnates, take a month off and let your body remember how to climb.

Tip: If you climb frequently, take one month off per year to enhance performance. That's right. Such down time will renew motivation, rejuvenate the body, and improve technical skills via the reminiscence effect.

Q. I just "tweaked" a tendon near the base of my left ring finger. Can I "climb through" this injury or should I take a some time off?

The short answer is to stop climbing and give it a few weeks of complete rest. Do this, and hopefully you'll prevent it from becoming a chronic injury.

Injury to the A2 tendon pulley at the base of the finger is ubiquitous among climbers. It can happen on a single strenuous move or over the course of many weeks. But once you've got it, this insidious injury can linger for months, especially if you try to "climb through" it. Time off is the only sure cure. A preemptive strike of a month off will usually arrest the condition.

"Ring" method of reinforcing the A2 pulley.

Granted, few climbers have the patience to take a full month off. However, noted climber/orthopedic surgeon Dr. Mark Robinson urges you to heed severe tendon pangs and swelling early on and embark on the following coarse of action: (1) Cease climbing until all pain and swelling are gone (maybe only a week or two if you catch it early). (2) Take two more weeks off. (3) Perform two weeks of low-resistance strength training such as squeeze devices, putty, and so forth. (4) Begin climbing on large-hold routes for up to one month. (5) Move on to large-hold steep routes like cave bouldering and such for one month, then back to full force climbing thereafter. Frequent icing and use of anti-inflammatory medicines early on (while swelling persists) may speed heeling.

"X" method of reinforcing the A2 pulley and protecting skin.

However, use beyond the first few weeks is of no value. This complete course of action may take up to six months in severe cases. However, it's a great investment in your long-term climbing health and capabilities. Return to climbing too soon and a series of recurrences is likely.

As you return to climbing, reinforce the injured finger with tape. A few snug turns of athletic tape around the base of the finger helps support the injured tendon and presumably decreases the chance of reinjury. Finally, the myth that "anti-inflammatories (for example, ibuprofen and aspirin) taken before climbing helps prevent finger injuries" is false—it can do just the opposite.

Tips for treating finger-tendon-pulley injuries:

Stop climbing until pain and swelling are gone, then take two more weeks off. Begin with light resistance training for two weeks, then start climbing on low-angle, big-hold climbs for one month. Progress to steeper climbs during the next month, then back full force beyond that if still symptom free.

Q. I'd like to build a home training wall. What is the most affordable, effective, and easy design to build?

An 8-by-12-foot 45-degree overhanging wall is an effective bare-bones rig. I'm aware of many such walls built in dorm rooms, one-room apartments, basements, garages, attics, and backyards. Vertical climbing distance is not important, just steepness. Savage three- to six-move problems are all you need to build power. Link up a few of these problems to train anaerobic endurance. Voilà, a sport-specific workout in the

comfort of your home!

Holds are important. Don't skimp on real rock—go for plastic. You'll thank God you did after just a few workouts! Seriously, the holds on your wall play a major role in how often and long you train. To start, buy a variety of holds from several companies to see what you like. Then just load up your wall with as many holds as you can fit in! Select holds with a fine texture (or use sandpaper to smooth high-texture holds) so your skin does not wear out before your muscles.

Home walls provide efficient workouts and are a blast! Begin by first building a 45-degree wall, then add on as space allows.

Since your wall is steep, favor medium-sized shapes with usable features while avoiding highly-detailed holds with many small edges (merely "bells and whistles"). Add some well-rounded pockets and small, yet comfy crimper edges for working contact strength. As a guideline, select hold sizes as follows: 10 percent tiny foot chips (real rock is okay here), 20 percent small crimp edges, 30 percent pockets, 30 percent variety of medium-sized holds and pinches, and 10 percent large buckets.

Now, find a few good training partners and exercise self-discipline in not using the wall daily. Train hard and smart and have fun!

Q. I would like to add some campus training to my workout. What type of regimen do you suggest?

There are two methods of campus training: the original dynamic "up-down-up" campus-board style and the "dynamic-up-only" modular-hold style. Whereas the former can be use effectively by elite climbers, the second style is what I suggest for you and other intermediate-to-advanced climbers. What follows is a primer on using the preferred latter method (a more comprehensive campus power training booklet is available for $5 from NICROS or the author).

The goal is maximum intensity, no-feet-on-the wall boulder routes up a 45-degree over-hanging wall. Three- to ten-move problems are ideal. Start in a sit-down position and end on a "good" hold that clearly defines the end. Do these "campus routes" slowly to work static lock-off strength, or quickly to develop upper-body power and super-recruit forearm muscle units for what Wolfgang Güllich called "instant power." Either way, the procedure is the same.

Up campusing on modular holds is less stressful and allows training of a variety of grip positions.

Begin with a comprehensive 20- to 40-minute warmup composed of stretching, self-massage of the fingers and forearms, a few sets of pull-ups, and general bouldering. Crescendo bouldering intensity as you near the end of the warm-up period. Take a 5- to 10-

minute rest, drink some water, and perform additional stretching before it's campus time!

Fifteen to thirty campus routes (as defined above) form the meat of your workout. Each route or attempt lasts only a few seconds, but always take a two-minute rest after each. This part of your workout will last between 30 and 60 minutes. Your first five routes should be "give me's" up a series of five to eight large holds. The next 10 to 15 routes (or attempts) should be new and maximal. If you fail on the first attempt, try it up to three more times (always resting two minutes between attempts). If you still have no success, memorize the route to try during your next workout and move on. Wind down your campus workout with 5 to 15 more campus problems of decreasing difficulty. Now is the time to attempt "flashes" of some of your favorite campus problems (wired) from past workouts. End the session when you begin to fail on "easy" or wired routes. Flogging yourself beyond this point has little training value, courts injury, and digs a deeper hole from which you must recover before you can train again.

Complete your workout with 10 to 20 minutes of "light" traversing, and two sets of reverse wrist curls. Cool-down bouldering should not pump your arms, but instead encourage steady blood flow to begin eliminating waste products from your muscles. Combine this with consumption of some high-GI foods or a sports drink to initiate and enhance recovery. Follow up with high-quality protein, nine hours of sleep, and at least two days off from training or climbing. Break any of these rules and you break the efficacy of the workout.

As a final note, recruit a positive, high-energy partner for these campus-training workouts (and for all climbing outings,

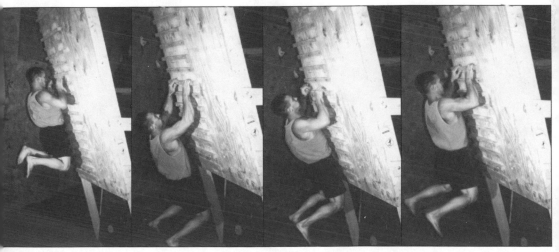

Drop-Down   Two-handed catch   Two-hand exploding   two-handed catch
                                         jump back up

Traditional up/down/up campus training rules supreme for recruitment and stress. Only extremely fit, advanced climbers should use this method.

if possible). Besides adding another creative mind to campus-route development, it will help enforce the campus protocol and increase motivation and intensity. But remember, when training near your limit there is a fine line you must not cross. End your campus workout immediately at the first sign of pain in the fingers or elbows.

GLOSSARY

The following is a compilation of some of the technical terms and jargon used throughout this book.

adaptogens: plant/herbal supplements believed to increase the body's nonspecific resistance; that is, aiding the immune system and improving physical and mental work capacity

aerobic(s): any physical activity deriving energy from the breakdown of glycogen in the presence of oxygen, thus producing little or no lactic acid, enabling an athlete to continue exercise much longer

aggro: short for aggressive

anaerobic: energy production in the muscles involving the breakdown of glycogen in the absence of oxygen; a byproduct called lactic acid is formed resulting in rapid fatigue and cessation of physical activity

anaerobic endurance: the ability to continue moderate- to high-intensity activity over a period of time; commonly called power endurance or power stamina

antagonist: a muscle providing an opposing force to the primary muscles of action

antioxidants: substances (for example, vitamins and minerals) proven to oppose oxidation and inhibit or neutralize free radicals

arousal: an internal state of alertness or excitement

back stepping: outside edging on a foot hold that is behind you while climbing a move with your side to the wall

beta: any prior information about a route including sequence, rests, gear, clips, and so forth

Biological Value (BV): a method for evaluating protein sources; a high BV protein source has a high percentage of nutrients actually absorbed from the human intestine as opposed to excreted

blocked practice: a practice routine in which a specific task is practiced repeatedly, as in working a crux move or sequence

bouldering: variable practice of climbing skills performed without a belay rope at the base of a cliff or on small boulders

campus (or campusing): climbing an overhanging section of rock or artificial wall with no feet, usually in a dynamic left hand, right hang, left hand sequence

catabolic: a breaking down process in the body, as in muscle break down during intense exercise, and so forth

chronic: long-term disorder; not acute

contact strength: initial grip strength on a rock hold

crimp grip: the most natural (and stressful) way to grip a rock hold characterized by hyperextension of the first joint in the fingers and nearly full contraction of the second joint

crux: the hardest move, or sequence of moves, on a route

deadpoint: the "high" position of a dynamic move where, for a moment, all motion stops

detox: to shakeout, rest, and recover from a pump

dropknee: an exaggerated backstep where one knee is dropped toward the ground whereas the other is pointing up, resulting in a stable chimney-like position especially on overhanging rock

dynamic move: an explosive leap for a hold otherwise out of reach

dyno: short for dynamic

eccentric muscle movement: muscle action in which the muscle resists as it is forced to lengthen

epicondylitis: inflammation of the tendon origins of the forearm flexors (medial) or extensors (lateral) near the elbow

ergogenic: performance enhancing

flagging: a climbing technique in which one foot is crossed behind the other to avoid barn dooring and to improve balance

flash: to climb a route first try without ever having touched the route, but with the aid of beta

flash pump: a rapid, often vicious, muscular pump resulting from strenuous training or climbing without first performing a proper (gradual) warmup

G-tox: a technique that uses gravity to help speed recovery from a forearm pump; it involves alternating (every 5 to 10 seconds) the position of the resting arm between the normal "hanging at your side" position and a "raised-hand position" above your shoulder

glycogen: compound chains of glucose stored in the muscle and liver for use during aerobic or anaerobic exercise

glycemic index: a scale which classifies how the ingestion of various foods affects blood-sugar levels in comparison to the ingestion of straight glucose

gripped: extremely scared

hangdogging: "climbing" a route, usually bolt to bolt, with the aid of the rope to hang and rest

heel hook: use of the heel on a hold, usually near chest level, to aid in pulling and balance

honed: in extremely good shape; with low body fat

hypergravity isolation training (HIT): a highly refined and specific method of training maximum finger strength and upper-body power via climbing on identical finger holds (isolation) with greater than body weight (hypergravity)

hypertrophy: enlargement in size (for example, muscular hypertrophy)

insulin: a hormone that decreases blood glucose level by driving glucose from the blood into muscle and fat cells

isometric: muscular contraction resulting in no shortening of the muscle (no movement)

kinesthetic: the sense derived from muscular contractions and limb movements

killer: extraordinarily good

lactic acid: acid byproduct of the anaerobic metabolism of glucose during intense muscular exercise

lunge: an out of control dynamic move; a jump for a far off hold

macro nutrients: basic nutrients needed for energy, cell growth, and organ function (such as, carbohydrates, fat, and protein)

manky: of poor quality, as in a manky finger jam or a manky protection placement

maximum strength: the peak force of a muscular contraction, irrespective of the time element

mental practice: practice in which the learner visualizes successful execution without overt physical practice

modeling: a learning technique where an individual watches, then attempts, a skill as performed properly by another person

motor learning: set of internal processes associated with practice or experience leading to a relatively permanent gain in performance capability

motor skill: a skill where the primary determinant of success is the movement component itself

motor unit: a motor neuron, together with a group of muscle cells stimulated in an all-or-nothing response

muscular endurance: the length of time a given level of power can be maintained

on-sight: when a route is climbed first try and with absolutely no prior information of any kind

open-hand grip: the safer and more powerful grip involving only slight flexion of the first two joints of the fingers

power: a measure of both force and speed (speed = distance x time) of a muscular contraction through a given range of motion (Note: Technically the term "finger power" is meaningless since the fingers normally don't move when gripping the rock.)

psyched: raring to go or very happy

pumped: when the muscles become gorged with blood due to extended physical exertion

random practice: a practice sequence in which tasks from several classes are experienced in random order over consecutive trails

recommended dietary allowances (RDA): quantities of specific vitamins, minerals, and protein needed daily that have been judged adequate for maintenance of good nutrition in the U.S. population, developed by the Food and Nutrition Board of the National Academy of Science

redpoint: lead climbing a route bottom to top in one push

reminiscence effect: the phenomena of enhanced motor skill and performance after an extended "time-off" period from climbing and training

schema: a set of rules, usually developed and applied unconsciously by the motor system in the brain and spinal cord, relating how to move and adjust muscle forces, body positions, and so forth, given the parameters at hand, such as steepness of the rock, friction qualities, holds being used, and type of terrain

send it: an emphatic statement to someone encouraging him or her to hang in and finish a route without falling

sharp end: the lead climber's end of the rope

shred: to do really well, or to dominate

skill: a capability to bring about an end result with maximum certainty, minimum energy, and minimum time

sport climbing: usually refers to any indoor or outdoor climbing on bolt-protected routes

spotter: a person designated to slow the fall of a boulderer, with the main goal of keeping the boulderer's head from hitting the ground

super recruiting: extreme, and potentially dangerous, power training utilizing "falling loads," which the muscles cannot lift but can "catch"

tendinitis: a disorder involving the inflammation of a tendon and synovial membrane at a joint

tendon: a white fibrous cord of dense, regular connective tissue that attaches muscle to bone

trad: short for traditional climber—someone who prefers routes with natural protection instead of bolts

training effect: a basic principle of exercise science that states that adaptation occurs from an exercise only in those parts or systems of the body stressed by the exercise.

transfer of learning: the gain or loss in proficiency on one task as a result of practice or experience on another task

tweak: to injure, as in a tweaked finger tendon

variable practice: practice in which many variations of a class of actions are performed; opposite to blocked practice

visualization: controlled and directed imagery that can be used for awareness building, monitoring and self-regulation, healing, and most importantly, as mental "programming" for good performances

wired: known well, as in a wired route

working: practicing the moves on a difficult route via toprope or hangdogging

Pyramid of Climbs to 5.10a

Fill in route name and date of redpoint.
One route per block.

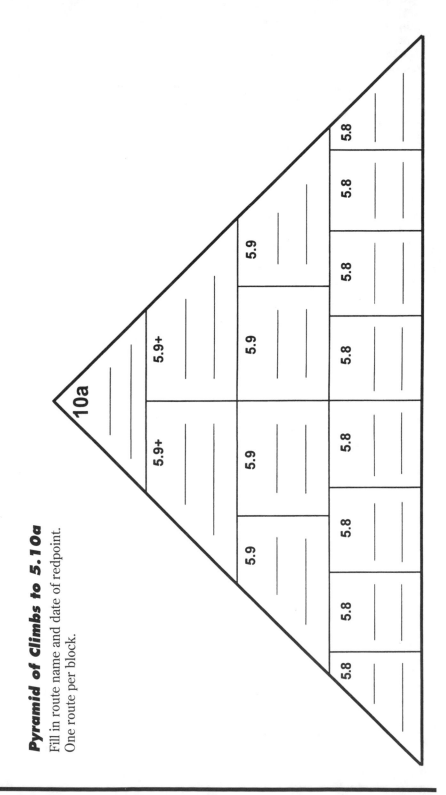

Pyramid of Climbs to 5.11a

Fill in route name and date of redpoint.
One route per block.

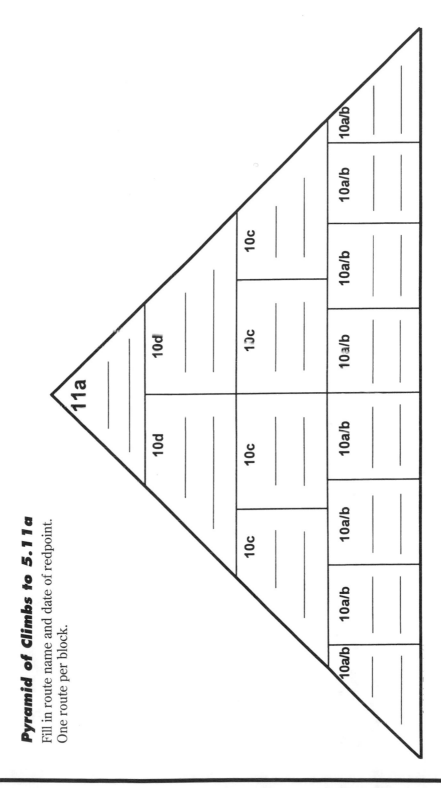

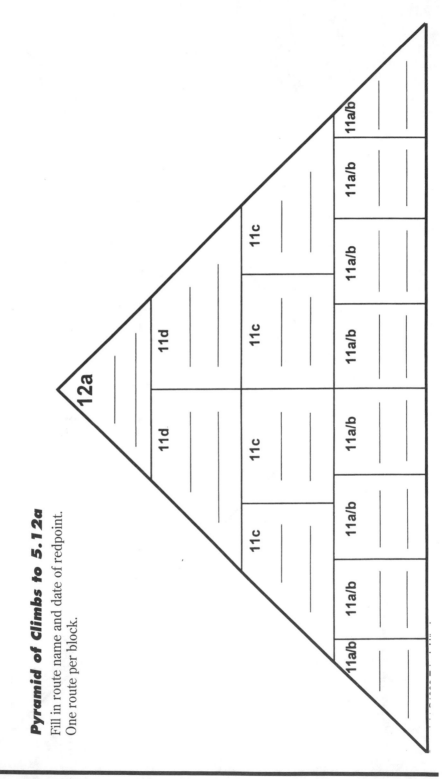

Pyramid of Climbs to 5.12a

Fill in route name and date of redpoint.
One route per block.

12a

11d   11d

11c   11c   11c   11c

11a/b 11a/b 11a/b 11a/b 11a/b 11a/b 11a/b 11a/b

Pyramid of Climbs to 5.13a

Fill in route name and date of redpoint.
One route per block.

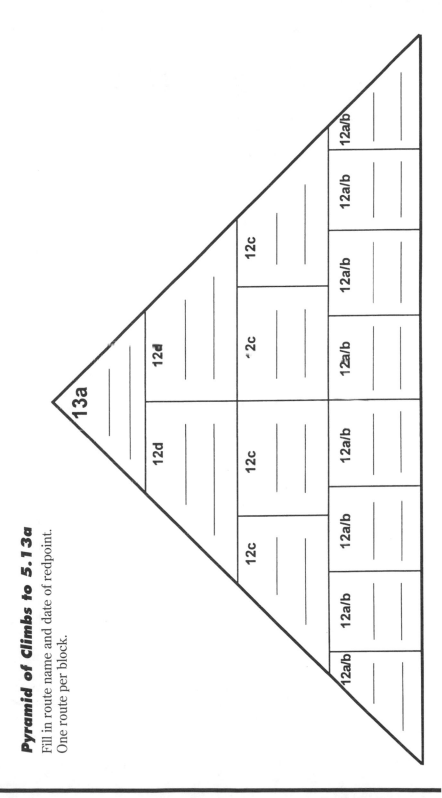

Fitness Evaluation and Questionaire

Use this fitness evaluation to periodically gauge your improvement in climbing fitness. Submit the results of your initial "self-test," and I will include them in a statistical study on which I am working (your name will not be necessary). Please return your evaluation and questionnaire (a copy is fine) to me as soon as possible. In return, I'll be glad to ship you a free "JUST SEND IT!" bumper sticker if you include a self-addressed stamped envelope.

FITNESS EVALUATION

This 10-part evaluation is strenuous. Perform a complete warmup before proceeding, then rest extensively between tests. If you like, take the test over the course of two workout days.

Test 1: One set maximum number of pull-ups. Do this test on a standard pull-up bar with your palms away and hands shoulder-width apart. Do not bounce, and be sure to go up and down the whole way.

Evaluation: Total number of pull-ups in a single go.

Results:_____

Test 2: One repetition maximum pull-up. Do a single pull-up with a 10-pound weight clipped to your harness. Rest two minutes, then add 10 more pounds and repeat. (If you are very strong, begin with a 20-pound weight and increase at 10- to 20-pound increments.)

Evaluation: The maximum amount of added weight successfully lifted for a single pull-up divided by your body weight.

Results:_____

Test 3: One-arm lock-off. Start with a standard chin-up (palms facing) then lock off at the top on one arm and let go with the other.

Evaluation: Length of time in the lock-off before your chin drops below the bar.

Results: Right arm_____ Left arm _____

Test 4: One set maximum number of Frenchies. Perform the exercise as described in Chapter 3. Remember, each cycle consists of three pull-ups separated by the three different lock-off positions that are held for seven seconds. Have a partner time your lock-offs.

Evaluation: The number of cycles (or part of) completed in a single set.

Results: _____

Test 5: One set maximum number of fingertip pull-ups on a 0.75-inch (19 mm) edge. Perform this exercise as in test 1 except on a fingerboard edge or doorjamb of approximately the stated size.

Evaluation: The number of fingertip pull-ups done in a single go.

Results:_____

Test 6: Lock off in the top position of a fingertip pull-up (0.75-inch or 19-mm edge) for as long as possible.

Evaluation: Length of time in the lock-off until your chin drops below the edge.

Results: _____

Test 7: Straight-arm hang from a standard pull-up bar. Place your hands shoulder-width apart with palms facing away.

Evaluation: Length of time you can hang on the bar before muscle failure.

Results:_____

Test 8: One set maximum number of sit-ups. Perform these on a pad or carpeted floor with your knees bent at approximately 90 degrees, your feet flat on the floor with nothing anchoring them. Place your thumbs on your collar bone and elbows out to the side.

Evaluation: Number of sit-ups you can perform without stopping. Do them slowly and in control (no bouncing).

Results:_____

Test 9: Wall split as described in the six key stretches box in Chapter 3. Be sure your butt is no more than 6 inches from the wall.

Evaluation: Position your legs so they are equidistant from the floor and measure the distance from your heels to the floor.

Results: _____

Test 10: High-step stretch as described in Chapter 3. Stand facing a wall with one foot flat on the floor with toes touching the wall. Lift the other leg up to the side as high as possible without any aid from the hands.

Evaluation: Measure the height of your step off the floor and divide it by your height.

Results:_____

QUESTIONNAIRE

1. Name _____

Address_____

City/State/zip _____

E-mail address _____

2. Age_____ Sex_____

3. Height_____ Weight_____ Percent body fat (if known) _____

4. Previous sports background

_____

5. Number of years climbing? _____

6. Preferred type of climbing (sport, trad, bouldering, big wall)? _____

7. Current on-sight lead ability (75% success rate at what level)? _____

8. Hardest redpoint (worked route)? _____

9. Are you currently doing sport-specific training for climbing? _____

10. Do you have a home climbing wall? _____

11. How often do you climb indoors (days per month)? _____

12. Do you belong to a climbing gym? _____ Which one?_____

13. Have you ever participated in a climbing competition? _____

14. Have you ever been injured while climbing or training for climbing?____

If so, describe? _____

15. Approximately how many days per year do you climb? _____

16. How many different climbing areas have you visited in the past 12 months?

_____

17. What are your goals in this sport?

_____

18. What chapter or part of *How to Climb 5.12* do you like best?

_____

19. What subjects would you like expanded upon in my next book?

_____

_____

20. Is there any particular expert climber you'd like to hear from or ask a question? _____

Send your Fitness Evaluation and Questionnaire to the address below. Include a self-addressed stamped envelope and we will promptly send you a free JUST SEND IT! sticker. Thank you!

Contact information:
Eric J. Hörst
P.O. Box 8633
Lancaster, PA 17604
e-mail: send512@horstnet.com
homepage: www.horstnet.com

References

Colgan, Michael. (1993) *Optimum Sports Nutrition.* Ronkonkoma, NY: Advanced Research Press.

Duchaine, Daniel. (1996) *Bodyopus.* La Costa, CA: XIPE Press.

Garfield, Charles A. (1985) *Peak Performance.* New York: Warner Books.

Harris, Dorothy V., and Bette L. Harris. (1984) *Sports Psychology: Mental Skills for Physical People.* New York: Leisure Press.

Kubistant, Tom. (1986) *Performing Your Best.* Champaign, IL: Leisure Press.

Livingston, Michael K. (1989) *Mental Discipline.* Champaign, IL: Human Kinetics.

Nett, Francis, and Jeff Carrol. (1995) *Protein Arithmetic.* La Costa, CA: XIPE Press.

Nideffer, Robert M. (1985) *Athlete's Guide to Mental Training.* Champaign, IL: Human Kinetics.

Phillips, W. Nathaniel. (1991) *Natural Supplement Review.* Golden, CO: Mile High Publishing.

Schmidt, Richard B. (1991) *Motor Learning and Performance, From Principles to Practice.* Champaign, IL: Human Kinetics.

Schmidt, Richard B. (1988) Motor Control and Learning, A Behavioral Emphasis. Champaign, IL: Human Kinetics.

Southmayd, William, and Marshall Hoffman. (1981) *Sports Health: The Complete Book of Athletic Injuries.* New York: Perigee Books.

Williams, Melvin H. (1989) *Beyond Training.* Champaign, IL: Leisure Press.